Finding *Hope* in Crisis

Devotions for Calm in Chaos

GRACE FOX

AspirePress

Finding Hope in Crisis: Devotions for Calm in Chaos
© 2021 Grace Fox
Published by Aspire Press
An imprint of Hendrickson Publishing Group
Rose Publishing, LLC
P.O. Box 3473
Peabody, Massachusetts 01961-3473 USA
www.HendricksonPublishingGroup.com

ISBN: 978-1-62862-992-7

All Scripture quotations, unless otherwise indicated, are taken from the Holy Bible, New International Version®, NIV®. Copyright ©1973, 1978, 1984, 2011 by Biblica, Inc.™ Used by permission of Zondervan. All rights reserved worldwide. www.zondervan.com The "NIV" and "New International Version" are trademarks registered in the United States Patent and Trademark Office by Biblica, Inc.™

Scripture quotations marked NLT are taken from the Holy Bible, New Living Translation, copyright ©1996, 2004, 2015 by Tyndale House Foundation. Used by permission of Tyndale House Publishers, a Division of Tyndale House Ministries, Carol Stream, Illinois 60188. All rights reserved.

Scripture quotations marked NASB taken from the New American Standard Bible® (NASB), Copyright © 1960, 1962, 1963, 1968, 1971, 1972, 1973, 1975, 1977, 1995 by The Lockman Foundation. Used by permission. www.Lockman.org

Scripture quotations marked ESV are from the ESV® Bible (The Holy Bible, English Standard Version®), copyright © 2001 by Crossway, a publishing ministry of Good News Publishers. Used by permission. All rights reserved.

Scripture quotations marked AMP taken from the Amplified® Bible (AMP), Copyright © 2015 by The Lockman Foundation. Used by permission. www.Lockman.org

Scripture quotations marked KJV are taken from the King James Version of the Bible.

Cover design by Sergio Urquiza; page design by Cristalle Kishi.

Cover photo: Take Photo/Shutterstock.com. Illustrations used under license from Shutterstock.com by lisima, inoha, Elena Medvedeva, Olga Koelsch, Galyna Gryshchenko, Sandra M, and Zhanna Smolyar.

Printed in the United States of America
020221VP

To

_____

From

_____

Date

_____

Contents

Our Weakness, God's Strength 10

God's Solution for Worry 12

Two-Word Prayers 14

Always on Time 16

Changed 18

Thrive 20

Let Go and Soar 22

Finding Courage 24

Faithful God 26

Asleep in the Storm 28

An Everywhere God 30

A Character-Building God 32

A God with Good Purposes 34

God Is in Control 36

Stand Still 38

Our Prayer Partner 40

Never Alone 42

Perfect Peace 44

Balanced 46

Remember 48

Sacrifice of Praise 50

Friends 52

Shield of Faith 54

Treasures in Darkness 56

Wisdom 58

Angels among Us 60

God Aches, Too 62

Fly Away or Stay 64

When God Doesn't Explain 66

Growth in Dark Places 68

Big Shoulders 70

Self-Talk 72

Seeing Beyond Our Pain 74

Accepting Help 76

No Surprises 78

Something New, Something Good 80

God Sees 82

Crisis of Belief 84

Prevent Stumbling 86

In His Time 88

Worship in the Fire 90

Not Alone in the Fire 92

A Trustworthy Friend 94

Hope in Action 96

Nighttime Thoughts 98

Escape Route 100

Jesus—Prince of Peace 102

Hold Your Peace 104

In Good Hands 106

Morning Joy 108

Good Father 110

Finding Joy 112

Tug-of-War Prayer 114

Life Saver 116

One Voice 118

To-Do List 120

Thankful 122

Shadows 124

Endless Supply 126

Fighting Our Giants 128

The Gift of Peace 130

Jesus Prays for You 132

Undefeatable 134

This Day 136

Healed from Shame 138

Refresh 140

No Separation 142

Deeply Loved 144

Mountain-Maker 146

Choosing Joy 148

Comfort Others 150

Rest 152

Praying God's Promises 154

Trading Worry for Songs in the Night 156

Wait 158

Moving Beyond Dismay 160

Snuggle 162

Tie a Knot and Hang On 164

God's Reality 166

Carried 168

Heart Care 170

Guard Your Mind 172

Our Strong Fortress 174

But God 176

On Your Side 178

El Shaddai 180

Leave Concerns Behind 182

Reflecting Jesus 184

Give God the Controls 186

Overwhelming Victory 188

Dear Friend,

Life can change in a nanosecond. Crisis strikes, and we wonder whether we'll survive the next hour, never mind the day. Our soul yearns for the storm to subside, for calm amid the chaos, for rest in our new reality.

We can barely think straight, let alone focus on anything beyond the situation at hand. It's easy, then, to set God's Word aside, but crisis is when we need it most. The Word reminds us that we're not alone because God's presence is with us. It promises his strength in our weakness. It reassures us that he consoles those who grieve. When trouble flips our world upside down, the Word rights us. Its living truths infuse us with hope.

I've written this little book with the prayer that it will bring encouragement as you walk through this hard place. Press pause for a minute each day to read from its pages. Inhale the Holy Spirit's peace. Exhale your worries and fear.

May I pray for you?

Heavenly Father, bless my friend with reminders of your presence during this difficult time. Supply comfort, wisdom, strength, physical rest—whatever's needed to rise above discouragement and fear. Bring your glorious purposes to pass. I pray in the power of Jesus' name, and I thank you in advance. Amen.

Know you are loved,

Grace Fox

Our Weakness, God's Strength

Each time he said, "My grace is all you need.
My power works best in weakness."
So now I am glad to boast about my weaknesses,
so that the power of Christ can work through me.

2 CORINTHIANS 12:9 NLT

Pause

When the idea for this book was born, I figured I'd had enough trials to make my authorship credible. Apparently, I was wrong. Seems I had to live a crisis while writing about finding hope in crisis.

First, the pandemic struck and my city became a hot spot with hefty restrictions. Then I cracked my tailbone. Minimizing pain while writing meant rotating between standing for hours and sitting on an O-cushion. Then a shoulder injury flared, and pain kept me from sleeping more than three hours at night.

To say I felt weak is a gross understatement, but that weakness forced me to rely on God. It became the portal through which his power brought this book into being.

Humanity often considers weakness a hindrance, but it's a blessing in disguise. It removes our self-reliance and provides an opportunity to experience God's power in new ways.

Ponder

In what area of your life do you feel weak? How might it be a portal to see God's power?

Pray

Lord, I lack strength today. Please make up for my lack with your infinite power.

"Character cannot be developed in ease and quiet. Only through experience of trial and suffering can the soul be strengthened, vision cleared, ambition inspired, and success achieved."

HELEN KELLER

11

God's Solution for Worry

*Do not be anxious about anything, but in every
situation, by prayer and petition, with thanksgiving,
present your requests to God. And the peace of God,
which transcends all understanding, will guard your
hearts and your minds in Christ Jesus.*

PHILIPPIANS 4:6–7

Pause

A popular song tells us not to worry. Be happy, it says. Easier said than done when your world is falling apart, right? But here's the thing: God also says not to worry, but then he tells us how to do this.

God's solution works like a mathematical equation. First, we have to choose not to dwell on thoughts that bring angst. Second, we pray. We admit our helplessness and acknowledge our need for God's help and wisdom. Third, we give thanks. We express gratitude for his presence, wisdom, unfailing love, and anything else that comes to mind. Doing so moves our focus from the problem to the Problem-Solver.

Saying no to anxiety + prayer + thanksgiving. That's God's solution for worry. And here's the outcome: peace that passes human understanding will guard our hearts and minds. Peace—not happiness that depends on our circumstances—stands like a sentry and refuses to let worry in.

Ponder

What can you thank God for in the midst of your crisis?

Pray

Father, please give me the ability to follow your solution so that I might experience your peace.

"Worry does not empty tomorrow of its sorrow, it empties today of its strength."

CORRIE TEN BOOM,
Clippings from My Notebook

Two-Word Prayers

*"LORD, help!" they cried in their trouble, and he saved
them from their distress. He led them from the darkness
and deepest gloom; he snapped their chains.*

PSALM 107:13–14 NLT

Pause

Crisis can drop us to our knees. We know that prayer is important, but sometimes it's hard to string two words together coherently, let alone an entire sentence. How can we pray effectively if we can't even think straight?

The writer of Psalm 107 describes several scenarios where people find themselves at wit's end. Some land there due to circumstances beyond their control. Some fall into dire straits due to their own poor judgment. Regardless, they're all in desperate need of divine intervention, and they all pray desperate prayers. Those prayers are neither lengthy nor eloquent, but they come from the heart. And they're short. Two words, to be exact: "Lord, help!"

The length and eloquence of our prayers has no bearing on God's ability to hear them or his willingness to answer. He knows our heart and hears the words we can't express. Two-word prayers spoken in sincerity catch his attention and draw his help.

Ponder

How does knowing that God hears the words you can't express bring hope?

Pray

Dear Father, thank you for hearing my simple, desperate cries.

"To pray is to accept that we are, and always will be, wholly dependent on God for everything."

TIMOTHY KELLER,
Prayer: Experiencing Awe and Intimacy with God

Always on Time

I waited patiently for the LORD to help me,
and he turned to me and heard my cry.
He lifted me out of the pit of despair,
out of the mud and the mire.

PSALM 40:1–2 NLT

Pause

I was kindergarten-age when I tried crossing a muddy road. My feet became stuck in the muck, and I yelled for help. I yelled louder upon seeing a concrete truck rumble toward me. A neighbor rushed to my rescue, not a moment too soon.

Sometimes I feel like my child-self, mired in tough circumstances about to get worse. I cry to God for help, and I cry again—louder—if rescue doesn't come immediately. Patience and panic don't dwell in the same heart.

I suspect that the psalmist exercised patience because he understood God's nature. Having a good grasp on God's wisdom, sovereignty, and love enabled him to trust

God's timing. He knew God would respond not a moment too soon or too late.

Such is our Rescuer God. Wise. Sovereign. Loving. He hears our cries, and he comes at just the right time.

Ponder

Identify one blessing you've received while waiting for God to answer your cries for help.

Pray

Lord, I know you will rescue me. Help me wait patiently.

"Have you entrusted everything concerning your case to Jesus? If you have, then the entire matter is sealed and delivered—in His resurrection. The message is this: As surely as Jesus rose on time, your triumph will be on schedule also. Lazarus's schedule probably seemed a day late to him, too."

JACK HAYFORD, *Moments with Majesty*

Changed

And we all, who with unveiled faces contemplate the Lord's glory, are being transformed into his image with ever-increasing glory, which comes from the Lord, who is the Spirit.

2 CORINTHIANS 3:18

Pause

It's inevitable—life's hard places change us. We cannot pass through the valley of suffering and emerge the same person. Our journey has the potential to either deepen us or destroy us, and we determine the direction it goes.

Compare the lives of two biblical women. Anna was married only seven years when her husband died. She spent the rest of her life worshiping God through prayer and fasting in the temple. At age eighty-four, she immediately recognized the infant Jesus as the Messiah, burst into praise, and told everyone about him (Luke 2:36–38).

Naomi lost her husband and two adult sons. In the aftermath of loss, she renamed herself saying, "Call me

Mara, because the Almighty has made my life very bitter" (Ruth 1:20).

God's intent is not that suffering makes us bitter. His desire is that it makes us better—kinder, gentler, wiser, stronger. His intent is that pain makes us more like Jesus.

Ponder

If someone wrote your story, what would you want written about your response to pain?

Pray

Lord, make me better. Make me more like Christ.

"We can do one of two things with suffering: we can absorb it and let it change us, or we can let it crush us. Suffering will change you, or it will crush you."

JENNIE ALLEN,
Restless: Because You Were Made for More

Thrive

So do not fear, for I am with you; do not be dismayed,
for I am your God. I will strengthen you and help you;
I will uphold you with my righteous right hand.

ISAIAH 41:10

Pause

I was twenty-four years old when I moved to Nepal with my husband, Gene. We studied the language for five months and then moved to a village far from Kathmandu. Gene spent nine hours a day at the hydroelectric power project where he worked. I stayed home.

Culture shock and loneliness overcame me. The day a six-foot snake slithered into my house nearly sent me over the brink. As I sat on Gene's knee that evening and cried, the most amazing thing happened. Over our shortwave radio came "Great Is Thy Faithfulness" sung in English. It was the first and only time I heard a Christian song on the radio during our time there. I knew that the Lord was with me and would help me not merely survive but thrive in my hard place.

The Lord knows where you are, too, and he will help you thrive there. It might take a little time, but keep the faith. He will meet you in your hard place.

Ponder

What would thriving in your situation look like?

Pray

Lord, please send tangible evidence of your presence with me.

"Through God's grace, he gives us a wealth of resources to bear any burden he allows. Therefore, if God doesn't empty our cup of suffering or take it from us, he will give ample grace (favor, kindness, ability) to bear it."

JENNIFER ROTHSCHILD,
God Is Just Not Fair: Finding Hope When Life Doesn't Make Sense

Let Go and Soar

But those who hope in the L{ORD} will renew
their strength. They will soar on wings like eagles;
they will run and not grow weary,
they will walk and not be faint.

ISAIAH 40:31

Pause

Two bald eagles flew past my window as I wrote today's entry. I set work aside for a few moments to watch the massive birds ride the wind. Using thermal currents to lift themselves heavenward, they embodied majesty and might. The sight of them soaring and circling higher and higher without even flapping their wings left me in awe.

Scripture says we become like eagles when we hope in the Lord. This means we acknowledge our need for his intervention in our situation and then trust him for the best outcome. In the process, we give him our fears and uncertainties. We surrender our expectations. We yield our desire for control.

Unloading these weights onto the Lord renews our strength and enables us to soar on the winds of adversity. We learn to view those winds not as a force sent to destroy us but as a means to experience God's supernatural power at work in us.

Ponder

What weights must you cast on the Lord so you can soar in his strength today?

Pray

Father, teach me to trust you implicitly for the best outcome.

"*Humbly let go*. Let go of trying to *do*, let go of trying to control ... let go of my own way, let go of my own fears. Let God blow His wind, His trials, oxygen for joy's fire. Leave the hand open and *be*. Be at peace. Bend the knee and be small and let God give what God chooses to give because *He only gives love* and whisper surprised thanks."

ANN VOSKAMP, *One Thousand Gifts: A Dare to Live Fully Right Where You Are*

Finding Courage

*I would have despaired unless I had believed that I
would see the goodness of the LORD in the land of
the living. Wait for the LORD; Be strong and let your
heart take courage; Yes, wait for the LORD.*

PSALM 27:13–14 NASB

Pause

Carole Lewis had many reasons to despair. First, she and
her husband suffered bankruptcy. Then her youngest
daughter was killed by a drunk driver and left three little
girls motherless. Hurricane Ike followed, destroying her
home and earthly possessions. Then her husband died,
and her son-in-law passed shortly afterward.

Carole faced one crisis after another without losing
hope. She clung to God for strength and trusted him
with confident expectation to come through for her.
Psalm 27:13–14 became part of the fabric of her life, and
courage became her trademark.

Courage can become our trademark, too. The key lies in believing God is sovereign and that he will redeem tragedy for good. Our role is to trust that he truly will do it and to wait for him to act even though it might take longer than we wish. He will never disappoint.

Ponder

What truth about who God is brings courage as you wait for him to redeem tragedy?

Pray

Lord, make courage my trademark. Give me patience to wait for you to bring good from the challenge I face today.

"The word of God gives strength and courage. I know this is true. Before my daughter died, I'd memorized one Bible verse a week for two years. After the accident, I recited those verses every day as I walked on a treadmill. They saved my life then and continue to carry me through every challenge I face."

CAROLE LEWIS, author of *Give God a Year, Change Your Life Forever*

Faithful God

Let us hold fast the confession of our hope without wavering, for He who promised is faithful.

HEBREWS 10:23 NASB

Pause

My eldest daughter was born with a heart defect and hydrocephalus—too much water on the brain. We were living in Nepal, and the medical system was inadequate for her needs. Doctors told us to return to America on the first available flight.

Because I'd had a Cesarean section delivery, the travel agent labeled me a medical high risk and refused to issue me a ticket. My husband wrapped our baby in a blanket and took her halfway around the world while I remained behind, not knowing whether I'd see her alive again.

"What are you doing, God?" I cried. "What do you want me to learn through this?" He answered by bringing the lyrics of "Great Is Thy Faithfulness" to mind. He didn't promise the outcome I wanted, but he promised to be faithful no matter what.

Hold fast to hope, my friend. You don't know how your story will end, but you can know with certainty that God will be faithful. Meditate on this truth, and let it bring calm to your chaos.

Ponder

Close your eyes. Inhale and thank God for being faithful. Exhale fear.

Pray

Father, I trust you because you are faithful—always have been and always will be.

"God keeps His promises. It's a major part of His immutable nature. He doesn't hold out hope with nice-sounding words, then renege on what He said He would do. God is neither fickle nor moody. And He never lies. As my own father used to say of people with integrity, 'His word is His bond.'"

CHARLES R. SWINDOLL,
Elijah: A Man of Heroism and Humility

Asleep in the Storm

Jesus was in the stern, sleeping on a cushion.
The disciples woke him and said to him,
"Teacher, don't you care if we drown?"

MARK 4:38

Pause

The perfect storm blew into my family's life on the day our eldest daughter was born. Doctors in Nepal couldn't address her medical needs, so an immediate return to the States became necessary. I remained behind for a week because my C-section disqualified me from air travel. Gene had no job awaiting him in North America. We had neither home nor car. And we had no insurance to cover neonatal intensive care costs. Waves of fear swamped our boat—fear for our baby's well-being, fear of an unknown future, and fear of financial insecurity. And that fear became the magnet that drew us closer to Jesus.

How could Jesus sleep in the storm? He knew everything was under control. We soon realized this was true as he provided for every need including coverage for hospital bills.

My friend, Jesus is fully aware of the storm you're experiencing and he knows there's no need for panic. Everything's under control. His control.

Ponder

Place your head on a pillow and take a needed rest. Let Jesus steer the boat.

Pray

Lord, if you can sleep in the storm, then so can I. Please help me rest.

"We can find ourselves in the middle of God's perfect will and in the middle of a perfect storm at the same time!"

DAVID JEREMIAH,
What Are You Afraid Of?

An Everywhere God

*So [Joseph's master] took Joseph and threw him into
the prison where the king's prisoners were held, and
there he remained. But the LORD was with Joseph in
the prison and showed him his faithful love.*

GENESIS 39:20–21 NLT

Pause

Joseph was a teenager when his jealous brothers turned
on him. Their actions thrust him into slavery in a foreign
country where he no doubt experienced culture shock.
Then a false accusation landed him in prison where his
captors bruised his feet in fetters and held his neck in an
iron collar (Psalm 105:17–19).

Where was God when Joseph's story went from bad to
worse? He was present with him in the cell. The writer of this
account mentions God's presence three times. Repetition
in Scripture indicates something significant. It's like a light
flashing to capture our attention. It says, "Don't blow past
these words. You need to understand their importance."

Suffering might cause us to question God's presence. Where is he? Has he forgotten me? Joseph's story reminds us of the truth. His situation seemed hopeless, yet God was with him in his cell. He's with us in our hard places, too, even when circumstances point to the opposite.

Ponder

How has God shown his faithful love in your situation?

Pray

Lord, thank you for your presence with me in this hard place.

"You are before me and behind me, above me and below me, around me and in me. You hem me in with your reassuring presence, whether I'm coming or going. It's a wonderful thing to ponder. Thank you for being my prepositional God."

TWILA BELK, *Raindrops from Heaven: Gentle Reminders of God's Power, Presence, and Purpose*

31

A Character-Building God

*Until the time came to fulfill his dreams,
the LORD tested Joseph's character.*

PSALM 105:19 NLT

Pause

We might think Joseph's jail time wasn't so bad. He was the warden's right-hand man enjoying free roam, right? That's true, to a degree. But let's not forget his time spent in fetters and an iron collar. Prisons were horrible places. How difficult his experience must have been! But God had a purpose for Joseph's pain.

God knew Joseph would someday be a key leader. Doing his job well would require integrity, knowledge, wisdom, and compassion. These qualities needed to be developed and honed. Prison became the place of preparation. The cell became his classroom. When the appointed time came, Joseph was ready.

Life would be easier if we could develop character through self-improvement courses. We'd rather forget the cell and forego the trials, but God knows how to best prepare us for the purposes we cannot see. Only he knows the road on which we travel and what lies ahead. Let's work with him and allow him to use this time to grow us into the people he wants and needs us to be.

Ponder

What character quality is God honing through your circumstances?

Pray

Father, use my pain for your highest purposes. Don't let it be in vain.

"Every adversity that comes across our path,
whether large or small, is intended to help us grow
in some way. If it were not beneficial,
God would not allow it or send it. …
He brings only that which is necessary, but He
does not shrink from that which will help us grow."

JERRY BRIDGES, *Trusting God*

A God with Good Purposes

*You intended to harm me, but God intended it
for good to accomplish what is now being done,
the saving of many lives.*

GENESIS 50:20

Pause

Joseph suffered rejection, slavery, and wrongful imprisonment in his first three decades of life. This would have been a lot for anyone to handle, but imagine how he felt knowing his brothers' role. A lesser man might have become hateful, consumed by a need to seek vengeance. But something set Joseph apart and empowered him to respond to his brothers as only a man of integrity could.

Joseph lived Romans 8:28 long before Paul penned it: "And we know that God causes all things to work together for good to those who love God, to those who are called according to *His* purpose" (NASB). These words applied can transform our attitude toward those who play a role in causing our pain. It changes our focus from what they've done to what God can do in spite of them.

Nothing can thwart God's purposes for us. No one can usurp his authority over us. He can overrule even when someone with evil intent has hurt us.

Ponder

Reflect on what "all things" looks like in your situation.

Pray

Lord, please turn the shards of my situation into stained glass.

"The truth of the matter is, Satan and God may want the exact same event to take place—but for different reasons. Satan's motive in Jesus' crucifixion was rebellion; God's motive was love and mercy. Satan was a secondary cause behind the Crucifixion, but it was God who ultimately wanted it, willed it, and allowed Satan to carry it out."

JONI EARECKSON TADA, *A Step Further: Growing Closer to God Through Hurt and Hardship*

God Is in Control

Finally, brothers and sisters, whatever is true, whatever is noble, whatever is right, whatever is pure, whatever is lovely, whatever is admirable—if anything is excellent or praiseworthy—think about such things.

PHILIPPIANS 4:8

Pause

Three weeks after my oldest daughter was born with significant medical concerns, I overheard two women talking about our situation. "I hope Grace doesn't blame herself for her baby's condition," said one. That thought hadn't yet crossed my mind, and thankfully it didn't stick. If it had, I'm certain I would have questioned and analyzed my way to a wrong conclusion.

Instead, I focused on Psalm 139:13–16. It says that God weaves our bodies together, and his workmanship is good. Whether God specifically designed my baby with hydrocephalus or whether he just allowed it was a question I couldn't answer, but I knew with certainty that I could trust his wisdom, goodness, and sovereignty.

We might never know with 100 percent accuracy what brought about difficult circumstances in our lives. Nonetheless, we can experience inner peace when we keep our minds anchored in the truth that God is in control and has purposes yet to be revealed.

Ponder

What thoughts about your circumstances need to align with Philippians 4:8?

Pray

God, show me your truth concerning my situation and help me anchor my thoughts on it.

"Though we may not be able to see his purpose or his plan, the Lord of heaven is on his throne and in firm control of the universe and our lives. So we entrust him with our future. We entrust him with our very lives."

MAX LUCADO,
America Looks Up

Stand Still

This is what the LORD says: Do not be afraid!
Don't be discouraged by this mighty army,
for the battle is not yours, but God's.

2 CHRONICLES 20:15 NLT

Pause

King Jehoshaphat knew his army was no match for the approaching enemy. He called his people to fast and pray, and he led them in seeking God's help. He probably expected God to tell him where to post his soldiers and when to attack, but the Lord took a different approach. God told the people to take up their positions and then stand still. This battle belonged to him, and he would accomplish the victory.

Sometimes God calls us to action. Other times he calls us to be still. We might find the latter strategy difficult, especially if we're prone to want to fix people and circumstances. We'd rather defend ourselves or rush to rescue someone in trouble. But he will give us the ability to stand down if he says we must let him fight the battle on our behalf. Our role is not to question his strategy but to trust his wisdom and his ways even if they don't make sense to us.

Ponder

What is God telling you to do in response to the battle you face?

Pray

God, help me learn to get out of the way and let you fight for me.

"God calls His people to celebrate Him with singing and playing, and then He promises to do a little drumming of His own, *on the back of the enemy!*"

TERRY LAW with JIM GILBERT,
The Power of Praise and Worship

Our Prayer Partner

In the same way, the Spirit helps us in our weakness.
We do not know what we ought to pray for,
but the Spirit himself intercedes for us
through wordless groans.

ROMANS 8:26

Pause

The mountains near my home are like magnets for winter sports enthusiasts. Skiers and snowboarders from around the world brave the elements to test their skills on the slopes. Unfortunately, some also test the safety boundaries that park authorities set, and they end up in trouble. Unable to help themselves, they call for assistance, and trained volunteers rush to their rescue.

Such is the Holy Spirit's intercessory ministry on our behalf when we find ourselves at a loss. He comes alongside to join us in that place. He feels our pain. He reads our thoughts. He hears the words we can't express. He knows every detail about our circumstances, and he initiates a supernatural rescue mission designed to bring us through them.

You might feel totally inadequate for the challenges facing you today, but be encouraged in knowing that you can call on the Holy Spirit to help you, and he will rush to your rescue.

Ponder

Identify one concern for which words fail. Ask the Spirit to pray on your behalf.

Pray

Father, I'm at a loss today. Please send the Holy Spirit to rescue me.

"Sometimes I am so tired and I can't pray. It's in these times that I need to lean on the Holy Spirit. We might not know what to say, but the Spirit knows. Who better to know what God's will is for our lives than the third Person of the Trinity?"

SARAH FRAZER,
6 Ways the Holy Spirit Prays for You

Never Alone

I will lead the blind by ways they have not known,
along unfamiliar paths I will guide them;
I will turn the darkness into light before them and
make the rough places smooth. These are the things
I will do; I will not forsake them.

ISAIAH 42:16

Pause

Jenny was widowed when a heart attack claimed her husband's life. Married more than forty years, they'd been inseparable. They enjoyed spending time with their kids and grandchildren, held leadership roles in their church, and practiced hospitality in their spacious home. Of the two, he'd handled their finances. Now she was alone.

Jenny's inner strength amazed me. She grieved her husband but not without hope. When I asked how she was doing, she said, "This journey is taking me on a road I've never traveled. Every twist and turn is unfamiliar, but I'll be okay because God is with me."

Crisis often brings change. It moves us from the familiar path to one we've never walked. We don't know our way, and we might feel lost at times. But we don't make this journey alone. The Lord is our guide and will never leave our side.

Ponder

How has your situation brought change into your life?

Pray

Lord, I will walk unfamiliar paths with confidence knowing you're right beside me.

"May you believe from deep within that God is with you, for you, and will never let you go."

SUSIE LARSON,
Blessings for the Evening: Finding Peace in God's Presence

Perfect Peace

You will keep in perfect peace all who trust in you,
all whose thoughts are fixed on you!

ISAIAH 26:3 NLT

Pause

My oldest daughter contracted meningitis when she was a year old. Two misdiagnoses led to a nightmarish monthlong hospitalization that included two surgeries. My baby's brush with death left me panicked more than once. I longed for peace, but it seemed unattainable at the time.

I wish I knew then what I know now: Peace is possible, and in greater measure than we might expect. In Hebrew, the word *shalom* means "peace." In Isaiah 26:3, the term is *shalom shalom*—"perfect peace." Perfect—flawless, complete, total.

Imagine experiencing total peace. No shred of worry, no trace of fear. No doubt, no dread, no sleepless nights or knotted tummies. If something sounds too good to be true, it usually is—except in this case.

God promises to give us flawless, complete, total peace, but there's one caveat. We must do our part by training our thoughts to stay where they belong. *Shalom shalom* comes when we keep our minds on him and trust him for the best outcome.

Ponder

On what are your thoughts fixed in this situation?

Pray

Father, please help me keep my thoughts on you, not on the situation at hand. Then fill me with shalom shalom— your perfect peace.

> "In the midst of depression, grief, or fighting any battle of the mind, no one wants to be told, 'Think positive thoughts.' We all know it's important to think positively. But how do we do it? We have to purposefully set our minds on truth. Thinking positively often requires digging deep and making choices that are contrary to our feelings."

> RACHEL WOJO, *One More Step: Finding Strength When You Feel Like Giving Up*

Balanced

Fixing our eyes on Jesus,
the pioneer and perfecter of faith.

HEBREWS 12:2

Pause

My husband and I do workouts using an online resource. We're often instructed to do a stretch that requires us to stand on one leg while bending the opposite leg at a ninety-degree angle and holding that ankle. "Focus your eyes on a stationary object to maintain balance," says the teacher. "You're less likely to fall."

Figuratively speaking, crisis of any sort can knock us off balance. Fixing our gaze on something—or better, someone—immovable prevents us from toppling. Jesus is that someone. He endured suffering for our sake so we can do the same without losing heart. His example inspires us to persevere. It encourages us to look beyond the hardship to the hope that lies ahead.

Jesus refused to give up or run away from suffering. He persevered to show us that standing strong in the face of difficulty can be done. Keeping our eyes on him and his example helps us maintain our equilibrium and keep going when heartache threatens to topple us.

Ponder

What fears or doubts are threatening to knock you off balance?

Pray

God, keep my eyes focused on Jesus' example. Give me strength to keep going.

"Sudden loss, besides leaving us hurt and bewildered, can leave us listing seriously to one side. … God's secure love and His sure promise to care for us are the perfect ballast; they provide stability without adding weight to our load. When our lives are filled with Jesus Christ and the security, worth, and identity he provides, the losses we experience cannot destabilize us."

SUSAN LENZKES, *When Life Takes What Matters: Devotions to Comfort You Through Crisis and Change*

Remember

And I said, "This is my fate; the Most High
has turned his hand against me."
But then I recall all you have done, O Lord;
I remember your wonderful deeds of long ago.

PSALM 77:10–11 NLT

Pause

I'm discovering how aging and memory loss go hand in hand. I draw a blank on my passwords. I forget people's names. I can't even recall my kids' phone numbers. Maybe you can relate.

Stress makes forgetfulness worse. We may have difficulty remembering to eat or where we've placed important documents. We might miss a scheduled appointment. Worse, we might forget that God is with us and has given us everything needed to face uncertainty with courage.

Forgetting about God's presence and empowerment leads to wrong thinking. We begin to believe we're in this situation alone and will never survive. Fear takes over, skews our perspective, and ties us in knots.

How are you doing in that regard? Have the day's concerns consumed your thinking? Have they led you to a fearful place? You can turn the tide. Recalling God's faithfulness in the past brings courage to the present and hope for the future.

Ponder

Recall an instance when God proved his faithfulness to you.

Pray

Father, make me quick to recall your faithfulness so wrong thinking cannot commandeer my mind.

> "Remembering isn't passive, it is an action that brings the power of Jesus into our lives. As we remember what He has done, it enables us to stop focusing on impossibility and instead focus on the God who does the impossible."
>
> From *The Power of Remembering*
> (eternalwall.org.uk)

Sacrifice of Praise

Therefore, let us offer through Jesus a continual sacrifice of praise to God, proclaiming our allegiance to his name.

HEBREWS 13:15 NLT

Pause

My husband and I spent eleven years working with a camping ministry that required us to raise our own financial support. Living by faith while raising three kids was not easy. Stress mounted when they approached college age. Things climaxed the week our second child left home. That's when unexpected car and dental bills cost nearly six thousand dollars.

Was God telling us to find a real, paying job? We prayed and fasted, and we sensed him say to stay put and praise him even in our lack. So, we did. We praised him daily for being our provider, our friend, our fortress, and more.

Praise didn't change our financial state; it changed us. Focusing on God's character snapped the chains of fear over financial insecurity, and freedom flooded us. Nearly two decades of faith-supported ministry later, that freedom remains.

Giving God a sacrifice of praise means worshiping him even in a hard place. It's faith-stretching, but it's the antidote for fear and paves the way to freedom.

Ponder

What three things can you praise God for today?

Pray

God, give me courage to offer a sacrifice of praise to you, and to do so with joy.

"God requires your sacrifice of praise, at precisely what seems like the worst moment, because it reveals Christ Jesus in your life."

TERRY LAW with JIM GILBERT,
The Power of Praise and Worship

Friends

Share each other's burdens,
and in this way obey the law of Christ.

GALATIANS 6:2 NLT

Pause

My friend Trudy ended the phone call and sat in dumbfounded silence. A mix of anger, shock, and disbelief made her nauseous. She'd be the first to admit she wasn't a perfect mother, but hearing her daughter yell, "You don't love me! You've never loved me!" broke her heart.

Trudy's thoughts spiraled into guilt, shame, and blame. She felt them dragging her into a deep, dark pit of despair, but she chose to resist. She called a wise friend and poured out her heart. That friend listened and prayed with Trudy. Her presence and kindness brought calm and clarity.

Our tendency in crisis might be to withdraw. We believe we can tough it out. We keep silent for fear of what others might say if they knew. Pride prevents us from seeking help when we need it most, and we suffer for it. Galatians 6:2 implies that everyone has burdens and no one is meant to carry them alone. It's okay to ask for help. That's what friends are for.

Ponder

Are you carrying your burdens alone? If so, think of a friend with whom you can talk and pray.

Pray

Lord, please give me discernment. With whom can I share the concerns on my heart?

"We need people who will reach out and hold our hands whenever we find ourselves walking in the dark. People who are quick to put our hearts at ease and swift to remind us how much we are loved. … They become peepholes through which we glimpse the kingdom of God, inspiration to become the best possible versions of ourselves even in the most difficult circumstances."

MARGARET FEINBERG, *Fight Back with Joy: Celebrate More, Regret Less, Stare Down Your Greatest Fears*

Shield of Faith

Take up the shield of faith, with which you can
extinguish all the flaming arrows of the evil one.

EPHESIANS 6:16

Pause

Crisis leaves us vulnerable to the enemy called *Fear*. It launches an attack in our mind, planting seeds of doubt about God's intent toward us and those we love. It takes our imagination hostage and forces it to places occupied by dread. It shadows our thoughts, filling them with darkness so we can't see our way. But God has equipped us to fight back using the shield of faith.

Roman soldiers did battle carrying door-sized shields that covered them completely and protected them from harm. We do battle carrying the shield of faith when we exercise trust in God and his nature, and his promises to be with us, to provide for us, and to strengthen us.

No matter what situation we face, God gives us enough faith to deflect Fear's assaults. We can stand against the enemy, not merely hoping to win, but confident that we will overcome. Faith in God and his power, wisdom, and love thwarts Fear's attempts to make us its victims. Faith protects us from its grip and makes us victors instead.

Ponder

Identify your greatest fear in your current situation.

Pray

Father, teach me to use the shield of faith to fight the enemy.

> "The enemy's attacks may be directed toward the vulnerable part of your life, but the shield of faith will protect you from them. You *can* resist him!"

> CHARLES R. SWINDOLL,
> *Why, God?*

Treasures in Darkness

I will give you hidden treasures, riches stored in secret places, so that you may know that I am the LORD, the God of Israel, who summons you by name.

ISAIAH 45:3

Pause

My husband and I took our youngest daughter caving one summer afternoon. We donned safety helmets with headlamps and then kissed the sunshine goodbye to descend into the damp darkness behind an experienced guide. This tested my grit. At times, rocks narrowed the route and forced us to squeeze through vertical passageways. Other times, we crawled. This was more challenging than I'd expected, and I began wishing I'd remained behind.

My attitude changed when we reached a cave filled with crystals. They sparkled like colored glass in our headlamps' light. Their beauty was unlike anything I'd ever seen. And to think I wished I'd stayed in a more comfortable place.

God has hidden treasures for us, but the route to experiencing their beauty is never easy. It takes us from our comfortable place into the dark, but we needn't fear because he's our guide. Stay close to him. Don't give up even when the way becomes difficult. The beauty that awaits will be worth it all.

Ponder

What glimpse of hidden treasure have you already caught?

Pray

Lord, give me courage as you lead me through the dark to the treasure hidden there.

"I believe that suffering is part of the narrative, and that nothing really good gets built when everything's easy. I believe that loss and emptiness and confusion often give way to a new fullness and wisdom."

SHAUNA NIEQUIST, *Bittersweet: Thoughts on Change, Grace, and Learning the Hard Way*

Wisdom

If any of you lack wisdom, let him ask of God,
that giveth to all men liberally, and upbraideth not;
and it shall be given him.

JAMES 1:5 KJV

Pause

"God, help! I don't know what to do." This was my plea when a treasured relationship broke. I wanted to talk it out, but the individual involved shut me out. My heart ripped, I felt, beyond repair. I needed wisdom—lots of it—to know how to respond.

Difficult situations require insight, but often our supply is insufficient. Thankfully we don't have to operate from our deficit. God commands us to ask—respectfully demand—that he give us what's needed to understand or make good decisions in life's hard places. But there's one caveat. The words "of God" imply an intimate coming alongside him. We're not to rush into his presence like a stranger asking for favors. He wants us to draw near and ask from a place of deep friendship and trust.

The word "giveth" implies one who habitually gives. When we meet the caveat, God never withholds his help. He opens his hand and generously answers our questions.

Ponder

For what do you need wisdom today?

Pray

Dear God, I need wisdom to know how to walk this journey well. I trust you to give it to me.

"True wisdom is found in trusting God
when you can't figure things out."

JONI EARECKSON TADA,
The God I Love: A Lifetime of Walking with Jesus

Angels among Us

*"Father, if you are willing, take this cup from me;
yet not my will, but yours be done."
An angel from heaven appeared to him
and strengthened him.*

LUKE 22:42–43

Pause

Unseen spiritual forces move among us. They're angels on assignment sent to care for God's children (Hebrews 1:14). But they're not golden-haired cherubs with rosy cheeks and Tinker Bell wings. Bible accounts say some struck terror into the hearts of those they appeared to. Others came disguised as ordinary people.

On the night of his arrest, Jesus prayed for release from his suffering. Then he surrendered his will to the Father knowing what lay ahead. His agony went unnoticed by his disciples, who'd fallen asleep a few feet away, but God saw. He sent a supernatural being to give Jesus supernatural strength to endure the suffering ahead.

Perhaps you've entertained angels unaware. A stranger buys your coffee, speaks the encouragement you need at that moment, or appears from nowhere and lends practical help. God hasn't left you to fend for yourself. Angels are among us, and some are assigned to you.

Ponder

Recall an instance when a stranger brought encouragement.

Pray

Father, thank you for sending your servants to care for me when I need it most.

"Believers, look up—take courage.
The angels are nearer than you think."

BILLY GRAHAM,
Unto the Hills: A Daily Devotional

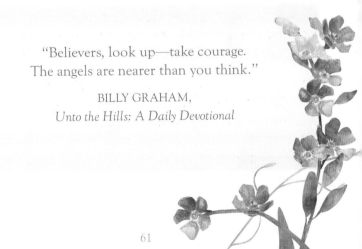

God Aches, Too

*This High Priest of ours understands our weaknesses,
for he faced all of the same testings we do, yet he
did not sin. So let us come boldly to the throne of our
gracious God. There we will receive his mercy, and we
will find grace to help us when we need it most.*

HEBREWS 4:15–16 NLT

Pause

My eldest—my only son—joined a sea-faring ministry for a
two-year commitment when he turned eighteen years old.
My heart broke the morning he left. None of my friends'
kids had done anything similar. Who could relate to the
pain I felt in saying goodbye to my child?

We attended church a couple hours later. The answer to
my question was written in calligraphy on a chalkboard:
"For God so loved the world, that he gave his only begotten
Son, that whosoever believeth in him should not perish, but
have everlasting life" (John 3:16 KJV). My friends couldn't
feel my pain, but God did.

Your circumstances have brought deep pain. Maybe sorrow or grief feel overwhelming right now. Family and friends care, but they can't fully understand. But God does. He knows exactly how you feel. You do not ache alone.

Ponder

Recall a time when God reminded you of his loving presence.

Pray

Father, thank you for aching with me.

"Jesus knows us fully. … He knows every nook and cranny of us. He knows us better than we know ourselves. And He also knows suffering on an intense, personal level. … He meets us in our downcast state and pours out grace upon us."

STEPHEN ALTROGGE, *The God Who Actually Does Know What You're Going Through*

Fly Away or Stay

I said, "Oh, that I had the wings of a dove!
I would fly away and be at rest.
I would flee far away and stay in the desert."

PSALM 55:6–7

Pause

Some theologians believe David coined today's key verse after he became Israel's king. Responsibilities and enemies stacked against him, and he longed to escape. He ached for his shepherding days. Life was simpler then. If only he could escape the palace, politics, and power struggles. If only he could run away and hide among the woolies. If only he could rest.

I can relate. Perhaps you can, too. We wish we could sprout wings. Fly away like a dove. Hide in a hole in a rock somewhere. Kiss stress, headaches, and sleeplessness goodbye. If only.

David poured out his heart to God, and then his tone changed. "But I will call on God, and the LORD will rescue me" (Psalm 55:16 NLT). Acknowledging his emotions was healthy. Depending on God to help him stay the course was right.

Our God will rescue us, too. He won't give us an escape pass, but he'll give us wisdom and strength to stay the course and do what's right.

Ponder

What makes you want to fly away and rest?

Pray

Lord, help me persevere in your strength.

> "God will often allow us to be in a situation with no possible solution. This is so we can discover that He is our solution. He lets us hit rock bottom in order for us to learn that He is the Rock at the bottom."

TONY EVANS,
The Power of God's Names

When God Doesn't Explain

"For my thoughts are not your thoughts,
neither are your ways my ways," declares the LORD.
"As the heavens are higher than the earth,
so are my ways higher than your ways
and my thoughts than your thoughts."

ISAIAH 55:8–9

Pause

My dad passed away one day after I arrived in Hungary to begin a two-week speaking tour across eastern Europe. Leaving the organizers in the lurch didn't seem right, so I chose to stay and fulfill my commitment. My family agreed.

The day of my dad's memorial service felt surreal. I was confident about my decision, yet my tears flowed. *God, why did you choose this timing? Couldn't you have waited two weeks so I could celebrate my dad's life with those who loved him?*

More than a decade has passed, and God still hasn't explained his timing. In the void, I choose to trust his ways. He's all-wise and all-knowing, and he's always working behind the scenes. His view is telescopic; mine is microscopic. Who knows, but perhaps in heaven, I'll meet an eastern European woman who responded to the gospel presented on that tour.

Ponder

What questions about your circumstances do you wish to ask God? Write them down. Now write "I trust your ways" above them.

Pray

Father, life doesn't make sense sometimes. Help me trust you when I don't understand.

"God will not permit any troubles to come upon us, unless He has a specific plan by which great blessing can come out of the difficulty."

PETER MARSHALL

Growth in Dark Places

*Those who sow with tears
will reap with songs of joy.*

PSALM 126:5

Pause

Georgia Shaffer was diagnosed with a recurrence of breast cancer at age thirty-eight. "There was no insulating shock, no numbness of disbelief," she says. "Fear was the only emotion I felt." She went into remission after aggressive chemotherapy, radiation, and a bone marrow transplant. But because she was too weak to return to work, she lost her job. Then she went through a divorce.

Georgia lost hope. She couldn't imagine her life ever improving. For many days, she sat on the steps outside her kitchen, crying and staring at her little garden. One morning her young son planted a few seeds. Over the next few days and weeks, Georgia watched as seedlings popped their heads through the dark soil and developed into strong, fruitful plants. The process restored her hope.

Although she was still in a dark place like a seed in the soil, she knew she wouldn't stay there forever. Healing would come, but it would be a process needing time. She would grow stronger with God's help and someday be filled with joy again.

Ponder

How does the word picture of a seed's growth resonate with you?

Pray

Lord, I trust you to give me everything needed to grow, blossom, and bear fruit.

"God brings the most exquisite flowers through dirt and dark times. But it doesn't happen overnight."

GEORGIA SHAFFER,
author and life coach

Big Shoulders

My salvation and my honor depend on God;
he is my mighty rock, my refuge.
Trust in him at all times, you people; pour out
your hearts to him, for God is our refuge.

PSALM 62:7–8

Pause

"Enough is enough! I'm done with the enemy trying to destroy my family. Do something already!" I don't usually talk to God like I did that day, but I was super frustrated. I felt like I'd prayed forever about the same thing without seeing answers. I was tired of watching the enemy gain ground in my loved one's life. I vented, and truth be told, I felt better.

Religion teaches that we must practice certain postures for prayer and say spiritual-sounding words. Relationship allows us to pour out our hearts to God and tell him how we really feel. And why not? He already knows anyway.

Someone once told me that God has big shoulders. He can handle it when we cry on him. He can deal with it when we tell him the truth about how we're *really* doing in the middle of our muck. We don't have to craft fancy words or make them sound sweet. He can handle our honesty.

Ponder

What would you really like to say to God today?

Pray

Father, thank you for letting me be honest with you.

> "Gut-wrenching questions honor God. Despair directed at God is a way of encountering him, opening ourselves up to the One and only Someone who can actually do something about our plight."

JONI EARECKSON TADA, *When God Weeps: Why Our Sufferings Matter to the Almighty*

Self-Talk

Keep me from lying to myself; give me the privilege
of knowing your instructions.

PSALM 119:29 NLT

Pause

Have you ever listened to the self-talk that runs through your mind? Losing my mobility for several months while living in a three-story townhouse meant having to hoist myself backward up fifteen steps to my bedroom every night. One night I caught myself saying, "I can't do this anymore." That became a defining moment for me.

I'd spoken a lie over myself. If I believed those words, I would lose hope. I'd quit trying to regain my health, and I'd suffer the consequences physically, emotionally, mentally, and even spiritually. From that moment forward, I chose to be more intentional about my self-talk, choosing words that reflected God's heart for me.

I encourage you to do the same. Become attentive to the way you talk to yourself in your thoughts. Measure your words against God's truth. If you catch yourself saying, "I can't do this anymore," readily acknowledge this as a lie. Then speak the truth: "I can do this in God's strength."

Ponder

Describe your usual self-talk. Do you unintentionally speak lies, or do you speak truth?

Pray

Father, make me aware of the words I speak in my thoughts and align them with your truth.

"Thoughts are real, physical things that occupy mental real estate. Moment by moment, every day, you are changing the structure of your brain through your thinking. When we hope, it is an activity of the mind that changes the structure of our brain in a positive and normal direction."

DR. CAROLINE LEAF,
Switch On Your Brain: The Key to Peak Happiness, Thinking, and Health

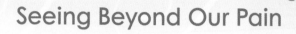

Seeing Beyond Our Pain

*For our present troubles are small and won't last
very long. Yet they produce for us a glory that vastly
outweighs them and will last forever!*

2 CORINTHIANS 4:17 NLT

Pause

My husband and I were in Poland when our son phoned from Canada at 6:30 a.m. He shared sad news: my father-in-law had died suddenly a few hours prior. Only sixteen months had passed since my dad's death while I was overseas. Now this.

I was sad about losing my father-in-law, but not being present with my kids to help them process another grandparent's death was even worse. I felt helpless and cheated. As I wrestled, God reminded me that he knew this would happen, and he would care for our kids. He would, in fact, use this to teach them to find their strength in him alone. He'd teach me to trust him with my loved ones' well-being. He would bring good by growing our faith.

God sees beyond what we see and knows infinitely more. He can use our pain to accomplish eternal good that far outweighs our temporal ache. Do we trust him?

Ponder

What are three things about your circumstances that God knew would happen?

Pray

Lord, my heart aches right now. Help me remember that you feel my ache, too, and you'll redeem it for something of eternal value.

> "The best we can hope for in this life is a knothole peek at the shining realities ahead. Yet a glimpse is enough. It's enough to convince our hearts that whatever sufferings and sorrows currently assail us aren't worthy of comparison to that which waits over the horizon."

JONI EARECKSON TADA,
Glorious Intruder: God's Presence in Life's Chaos

Accepting Help

When Moses' hands grew tired, they took a stone and put it under him and he sat on it. Aaron and Hur held his hands up—one on one side, one on the other— so that his hands remained steady till sunset.

EXODUS 17:12

Pause

Battles are rarely won when fought alone. Satan wants us to believe otherwise. He knows that, on our own, we become easy prey. He encourages us to isolate ourselves by putting thoughts into our mind such as, *What will other people think if they learn my family's a mess? What will happen if others discover my past failures? What will they think of me if I ask for help?*

Moses was a great leader, but he needed help to fight his battles. He could have determined to win the war alone or die trying. Instead, he allowed his friends to come alongside and literally lend a hand.

Admitting we need help might hurt our pride. Accepting help can be difficult, too. It means releasing control and letting others take charge. Doing so can be tough, but it might be necessary. Battles are fought and won by armies, not individuals.

Ponder

Who might hold your hands up as you fight this battle?

Pray

Father, make me willing to admit I need help and then to accept it.

> "You need someone to lift your spirits. You need someone to look you in the face and say, 'This isn't the end. Don't give up. There is a better place than this. And I'll lead you there.'"
>
> MAX LUCADO,
> *Traveling Light: Releasing the Burdens*
> *You Were Never Intended to Bear*

No Surprises

We can make our plans,
but the LORD determines our steps.

PROVERBS 16:9 NLT

Pause

I woke one morning in March 2020 assuming I knew what lay ahead. I was wrong. By day's end, the pandemic had forced the cancellation of my spring speaking engagements, a visit to my daughter's home, and our annual missionary staff conference in Poland. Traveling was banned, and Gene and I isolated ourselves in our sailboat. Whoever could have guessed life would take such a turn? I might have panicked had it not been for a phrase that replayed in my head: "This was no surprise to God."

The unexpected swoops in and changes everything in a heartbeat. Panic can so easily grip us if the control we've assumed for our lives is suddenly snatched away. But when the Lord is our shepherd, he takes responsibility for our well-being. Nothing happens to us that he does not allow or ordain. We can rest assured that everything will be okay.

The new plans won't look like what we expected, but that's alright. The Lord, in his wisdom and goodness, is changing them for our good and his glory.

Ponder

Look at your calendar. Invite the Lord to take charge over it.

Pray

God, teach me to trust you implicitly when my plans change.

"God is already prepared for everything you're going to face tomorrow, next week, and next month. What the future holds may surprise us, but it doesn't surprise God. Nothing ever catches him by surprise or makes him say, 'Oh, really?'"

RICK WARREN,
Nothing Surprises God

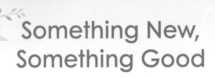

Something New, Something Good

When he had said this, Jesus called in a loud voice,
"Lazarus, come out!" The dead man came out,
his hands and feet wrapped with strips of linen,
and a cloth around his face.

JOHN 11:43–44

Pause

Lazarus was dead. His sisters had begged Jesus to come to his aid before it was too late, but he'd ignored their pleas. Or so they thought. Oh, the questions they must have asked: "Where is Jesus? Why hasn't he come? Doesn't he care?" They buried their hope with their brother. To them, death marked the end. To Jesus, it marked the start of something good. Many people came to faith as a result of circumstances that appeared disastrous.

God's perspective is vastly different from ours. We develop our own ideas of what our circumstances should look like and assume he'll agree because, after all, he loves us. He wants what's best for us, right?

Sometimes our circumstances fall into place. Sometimes they fall apart. Or so we think. In truth, God is at work in ways we cannot see. We think we've reached the end, but in truth, he's starting something new.

Ponder

How might your perspective about your circumstances differ from God's?

Pray

Father, help me view my circumstances through your eyes. Use my pain to accomplish eternal purposes.

> "The future may look a little foggy. It may look a little troublesome. You might have said, 'God, I can't see any good coming.' Here's what I've discovered. After God promised something, it doesn't make any difference what I feel or what I see, because God promised to make 'all things work together for good' (Romans 8:28). I trust with my life that He will do what He said."
>
> CHARLES STANLEY, *God Is in Control: An Unshakable Peace in the Midst of Life's Storms*

God Sees

[Hagar] gave this name to the LORD who spoke to her:
"You are the God who sees me," for she said,
"I have now seen the One who sees me."

GENESIS 16:13

Pause

Hagar was an Egyptian slave belonging to Abram and Sarai. Hers was a heartbreaking story. Used and abused by her mistress, she decided to escape and head for home. Exhausted, scared, and alone, she stopped to rest beside a spring. That's when God showed up. "Hagar," he said.

Hagar couldn't remember the last time she'd heard her name. She was only a slave. She was used to no one knowing her name or truly seeing her. No one cared about her well-being. At least that's the truth she'd come to believe. But that truth was not reality.

The reality was that God saw Hagar in her deepest moment of need. He sees you, too. You might feel exhausted, scared, and all alone. Maybe you feel invisible to everyone around you. But *El Roi*—"the God who sees"—knows your name and where you are. He's closer than you think.

Ponder

El Roi sees you and cares about your situation right now, right where you are. Let this truth sink into your thoughts.

Pray

Father, I know you see me. Open my eyes to see you, too.

"I want you to live in confidence that when God looks at you, He sees beauty. He sees value. He sees hope. And that even when you're hiding, or when you're so beaten down you can't see anything clearly, He's still hard at work, crafting a beautiful future of relationship with Him and with others."

TAMMY MALTBY,
The God Who Sees You: Look to Him When You Feel Discouraged, Forgotten, or Invisible

Crisis of Belief

Whom have I in heaven but you?
And earth has nothing I desire besides you.

PSALM 73:25

Pause

Lucinda's life was filled with friends and ministry, but her heart felt empty. In her early thirties, she often felt all alone. She longed for someone special to love who would love her in return. She prayed, asking God to answer her ache to be a wife and mother. "Your will be done," she added at the end.

Over time, Lucinda recognized that only God could satisfy her deepest longings and loving him would bring the greatest joy. She acknowledged that her journey of experiencing God as enough would come with moments of loneliness and even despair. She claimed his strength and indwelling power so she could move forward each day doing the next right thing and being the woman he created her to be. Surrendering her dreams to him gave her freedom to embrace a hope-filled future.

A crisis of belief comes when we must choose whether or not to trust the Lord to meet every need. Our choice reveals what we believe to be true about him and determines the direction our lives take.

Ponder

What's your crisis of belief in your situation?

Pray

Lord, I surrender my dreams to you. I choose to trust.

"What do we do when God's answer to our prayers doesn't look like what we've envisioned? We keep trusting the one who is sovereign and loves us. We love him more and more each day, moving forward in answer to his calling. And he makes us soul strong."

LUCINDA SECREST MCDOWELL,
Soul Strong: 7 Keys to a Vibrant Life

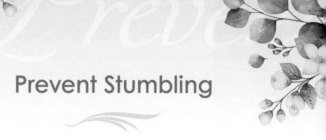

Prevent Stumbling

Great peace have those who love your law,
and nothing can make them stumble.

PSALM 119:165

Pause

It was dark and the dock was slippery when Gene and I returned from an overseas ministry trip. I was wearing a twenty-two-pound backpack and pulling a carry-on bag. Suddenly my left ankle twisted, and I went down. The weight on my back pushed me flat into the wood planks. Amazingly, my only injury was wounded pride.

Realizing how easily I can stumble encourages me to take extra precautions, especially on dark, rainy nights. The same is true in the spiritual realm. We can so easily tumble into the pit of doubt, fear, or self-pity when darkness falls and rain pours. That's where we lose perspective and doubt God's integrity.

We safeguard ourselves from falling by walking in God's truth. For instance, we read about casting our cares on the Lord, and then we do it. We hear about his faithfulness and choose to trust him. The more we walk in truth, the more peace and hope we experience and the less likely we are to stumble into despair.

Ponder

What's one action you can take to protect your heart from stumbling into fear?

Pray

God, help me readily identify wrong thinking that will trip me. Teach me to walk in your truth.

"Sometimes the wisdom of God will be a bitter herb to you. It will be contrary to the way you want to do things or the way you want to experience life. But if you will swallow that bitter pill—or, in other words, go ahead and DO what you know to do, no matter how hard it is and no matter how much you have to ENDURE—then you'll find yourself in a position to be resurrected by God with great victory!"

LARRY LEA, *Wisdom: The Gift Worth Seeking*

In His Time

He got up, rebuked the wind and said to the waves,
"Quiet! Be still!" Then the wind died down
and it was completely calm.

MARK 4:39

Pause

We'd invited friends for an overnight sailing trip. We motored up the river toward open water, and that's when things turned wild. Tide and wind moved in opposite directions and created wild waves that rocked our forty-eight-foot boat like a bucking bronco.

Green from nausea, I inched inside to catch apples and oranges that were now rolling back and forth on the salon floor. That's when I had a little but lively chat with God. "Help! Stop the wind! You did it once; do it again!" I wanted him to just speak a word and calm the sea right then and there. He could have done so, but instead, he took us through the waves to a safe harbor.

We can't begin to understand why God answers cries for help in so many different ways, but we do know that he is wise and good. Sometimes he rescues us from distress quickly; other times, he waits. Let's trust his methods. He makes no mistakes.

Ponder

How does it make you feel when God answers your prayers differently than you wish?

Pray

God, I'm grateful that your methods and timeline for answering my prayers is always good.

"To trust God is to trust His timing. To trust God is to trust His way. God loves me too much to answer my prayers at any other time than the right time and in any other way than the right way. In the quietness of all that doesn't feel right, this truth does."

LISA TERKEURST,
It's Not Supposed to Be This Way: Finding Unexpected Strength When Disappointments Leave You Shattered

Worship in the Fire

If we are thrown into the blazing furnace, the God we serve is able to deliver us from it, and he will deliver us from Your Majesty's hand. But even if he does not, we want you to know, Your Majesty, that we will not serve your gods or worship the image of gold you have set up.

DANIEL 3:17–18

Pause

"Worship the golden idol or else." The king's command became a crisis of belief for Shadrach, Meshach, and Abednego. Could they trust God to save them from the fiery furnace if they disobeyed? They knew the answer was yes, but they also knew his plans might differ from their hopes. What if they chose to honor him but he chose the fire for them?

The Jewish trio faced their crisis with bold faith: "Even if he does not spare us from the furnace, we will not serve any other gods." Their courage inspires us to bold faith, too.

We know God can deliver us from our painful circumstances. But even if he does not, let's not doubt his goodness or love. Let's trust him even if the heat increases. He'll be with us and will bring us through it to an outcome that will reveal his glory.

Ponder

Complete the sentence: "I will trust God even if _____."

Pray

God, help me worship you even if the heat increases.

"God is God. He knows what he is doing.
When you can't trace his hand, trust his heart."

MAX LUCADO,
Grace For the Moment:
Inspiration for Each Day of the Year

Not Alone in the Fire

*When you pass through the waters, I will be with you;
and when you pass through the rivers, they will not
sweep over you. When you walk through the fire, you
will not be burned; the flames will not set you ablaze.*

ISAIAH 43:2

Pause

God could have prevented Shadrach, Meshach, and Abednego from being thrown into the fiery furnace, but he did not. In what seems a cruel twist, he allowed soldiers to toss them into the furnace and turn up the heat seven times. Perhaps it looked like he had abandoned them in their crisis, but the truth soon became evident. The king, who was watching them, said, "Look! I see four men walking around in the fire, unbound and unharmed, and the fourth looks like a son of the gods" (Daniel 3:25).

We can't even pretend to understand why God allows us to experience times of intense suffering. Why doesn't he lead us around difficulties rather than through them? But this we do know: he walks through our fire with us and won't allow the flames to consume us. The fire burns hot and hotter and refines us while his presence keeps us from harm.

Ponder

What evidence do you have of God's presence with you in this fiery trial?

Pray

Father, use my circumstances to reveal yourself to those watching.

"If you remember with grateful amazement that Jesus was thrown into the ultimate furnace for you, you can begin to sense him in your smaller furnaces with you."

TIMOTHY KELLER,
Walking with God through Pain and Suffering

A Trustworthy Friend

*Then Jesus said, "Come to me, all of you
who are weary and carry heavy burdens,
and I will give you rest."*

MATTHEW 11:28 NLT

Pause

I was waiting to catch a train in eastern Europe when a
slight man dressed in ragged clothes approached me.
He motioned to my suitcase as though offering to carry
it. My instinct said, "Don't trust him." But the Polish friend
with me nodded.

The moment the train arrived, the man scooped up my
suitcase and climbed the steps. Once on board, he set my
bag down and opened his palm for payment.

I chose to trust a stranger. I accepted his offer to carry
my physical burden and paid him for doing it. Jesus offers
to carry our weight of another type for free. You'd think
we'd eagerly hand it over. Instead, we hesitate or insist on

carrying it ourselves. Why? Because we're not sure we can trust him and his intent toward us.

Jesus is no suspicious-looking stranger. He's our friend. Our *best* friend who always has our best interest in mind, and he is totally trustworthy.

Ponder

Have you trusted Jesus with your deepest pain? If not, why?

Pray

God, help me trust you more. Carry my concerns and give me rest.

"We're foolish unless we always trust Him with our destiny. Present trials, suffering, or tragedy may often seem the end—or cause us to wish it were. Yet the Father knows this period isn't the end of a sentence, but a connecting point in the completion of the masterpiece which is His whole story for us."

JACK HAYFORD,
Moments with Majesty

Hope in Action

*You who have made me see many troubles and
calamities will revive me again; from the depths of
the earth you will bring me up again. You will
increase my greatness and comfort me again.*

PSALM 71:20–21 ESV

Pause

Pam and Bill Farrel were beyond exhausted. Besides trying to sell their home and downsize, Bill was caring for his parents, who lived seven hours away. Pam was writing a Bible study and managing their marriage ministry. Stress rose; savings dwindled.

One day they fell on their faces before God and wept, pleading with him to act on their behalf. They drew hope from the promises in Psalm 71:20–21—you will revive me, bring me up, increase my greatness, and comfort me.

Pam drew a pair of glasses in her art Bible and wrote the verses across the picture. For months, she recited them every time she put on her glasses. Prayerful persistence paid off.

God fulfilled four promises for the Farrels. He'll do the same for you. Sometimes he acts quickly; other times, not so much. Don't lose heart. Be prayerfully persistent. Be patient, and watch him work on your behalf.

Ponder

What promise has God given you in this situation?

Pray

Lord, I believe you will fulfill your word. Help my unbelief.

> "Hope is a verb. Hope leans in and looks up. Hope is waiting expectantly for God to show up and show off for your good and His glory."
>
> PAM FARREL,
> author of *Discovering Hope in the Psalms: A Creative Bible Study Experience*

Nighttime Thoughts

*I reflect at night on who you are, O Lord;
therefore, I obey your instructions.*

PSALM 119:55 NLT

Pause

Negative thoughts and lies often come knocking at nighttime. The same happens when darkness envelops us in the night of the soul. Our imagination takes us to unwelcome places. Reflecting on who God is changes everything. I discovered this to be true after a broken engagement.

I began memorizing Bible verses and reviewed them while lying in bed at night. Meditating on God's sovereignty renewed my confidence that he was in control. It brought hope that my future would turn out well despite changed plans. Meditating on his love helped free me from believing I was unlovable. Focusing on his justice empowered me to forgive and release my offender into his hands. If I'd allowed negative thoughts to dwell in my mind as I fell asleep, I'm certain I would have become an angry, vengeful woman.

Where do your thoughts take you in the darkness? Don't let them be the boss of you. Take control and direct them to a life-giving place. Reflect on scriptures that remind you of who God is, and you'll blossom in this hard place.

Ponder

Choose one facet of God's character and meditate on it tonight.

Pray

Father, take control of my mind. Train my thoughts to think more on you.

"I want to shape my world around God's truth because I know as a scientist and a believer, paying attention to my thoughts and purposefully focusing my mind leads to great transformations."

DR. CAROLINE LEAF,
Switch on Your Brain: The Key to Peak Happiness, Thinking, and Health

Escape Route

Your road led through the sea, your pathway through the mighty waters—a pathway no one knew was there!

PSALM 77:19 NLT

Pause

The Israelites had reached the end. The Red Sea stretched before them and the Egyptian army approached from behind. There was no escape. Clearly, God brought them there to die and then abandoned them. They could think of no other explanation.

Their minds changed when the wind began to blow and the waves turned to walls. At the exact moment they needed it most, an escape route appeared. A dry path through the middle of the Red Sea led them to safety. Who would have guessed?

Perhaps, like the Israelites, you feel like you've reached the end. You see no options, no escape. Do not lose heart, my friend. Do not, in desperation, try to create your own way out. God did not lead you here to perish. He has prepared a path for your escape. You don't see it yet, but it's there. He has made a way where there appears to be none.

Ponder

Visualize the path through the Red Sea. Praise God for being the way-maker.

Pray

Father, I believe you've made a way of escape. Help me be patient until you reveal it to me.

"Trying to get through life on your own limited strength, knowledge, and resources leads to futility and a loss of hope. But in God's economy, getting to the end of yourself is the beginning of hope."

HENRY CLOUD and JOHN TOWNSEND,
What to Do When You Don't Know What to Do:
8 Principles for Finding God's Way

Jesus—Prince of Peace

*I have told you all this so that you may have peace
in me. Here on earth you will have many trials
and sorrows. But take heart,
because I have overcome the world.*

JOHN 16:33 NLT

Pause

My best childhood friend and I reunited after more than
thirty years apart. Sadly, she was in hospice battling cancer.
Time was short so we bypassed small talk. Our conversation
dove directly into all things Jesus. We shared stories of how
he'd helped us over the years. We spoke about having
learned to live the truths he taught. Best, we talked about
the hope of heaven and of meeting Jesus face-to-face.

My girlfriend had placed her faith in Jesus for salvation
decades prior. Her love for him had deepened over time.
Now, in the valley of the shadow of death, her courage
manifested his presence and her countenance reflected
his peace.

Trials and sorrows are inevitable. Tears flow, but an underlying peace is possible in the midst of them if we know the one who conquered pain and death. Jesus is the prince of peace. When we invite him into our life and choose to trust him, he rules over our circumstances and his comfort reigns in our hearts.

Ponder

Invite Jesus to reveal himself to you through your situation.

Pray

Father, calm my anxious heart and fill me with your peace.

"Peace is one of the gifts that God offers us through Jesus Christ. ... Christ's peace is not a passive quality that shuts our eyes to the harsh reality, but creates a positive approach to life, based on the belief in the trustworthiness of God."

SOLLY OZROVECH,
Grace for Today: One-Minute Devotions

Hold Your Peace

The LORD shall fight for you,
and ye shall hold your peace.

EXODUS 14:14 KJV

Pause

When a serious conflict arose within the church that Maggie and her husband pastored, they did their best to resolve it. One individual resisted all their efforts. They reached out to him, but he twisted their words and used them against the couple. Every attempt toward resolution made matters worse, and the situation led to litigation.

Maggie sought hope and direction in God's Word. He impressed Exodus 14:14 on her heart. In context, Moses spoke these words to the panicked Israelites as they stood between the Red Sea and the Egyptian army. They felt certain the enemy would destroy them, but God reassured them that he would fight for them. They only needed to be silent. Maggie felt God giving her the same directive. He would be their advocate. Peace would reign if they held their peace.

That's easier said than done when our reputation is being destroyed. Or when others lie about us. Or when someone makes wrong assumptions about us and treats us accordingly. Our tendency is to defend ourselves, but God says otherwise. Stay calm, and let him fight the battle.

Ponder

What does "hold your peace" look like in your situation?

Pray

Father, help me stay calm and keep my lips sealed.

"God holds the future, and because of his presence, you can hold your peace."

MAGGIE WALLEM ROWE,
This Life We Share

In Good Hands

Into your hands I commit my spirit;
deliver me, Lord, my faithful God.

PSALM 31:5

Pause

Numerous dots had to connect when it became apparent that God was leading us to move full-time aboard a sailboat. We had to find a suitable boat, secure finances, purge our belongings, and find a place to moor it despite there being a seven-year waiting list for live-aboard space. We had eight weeks to get it done, and I was writing a book under deadline at the time. To say I was overwhelmed is a massive understatement. Every morning I'd wake and pray, "Lord, help! Take responsibility for this. I can't do this on my own."

Remembering who the Lord is goes a long way in delivering us from fear and stress. He is Jehovah—the eternal God infinite in power, wisdom, goodness, and faithfulness. He rules the world, yet he knows the number of hairs on our head. Nothing is impossible for him.

It may seem sometimes as though God gives us more than we can handle. I believe that's true. But I also believe there's nothing he cannot handle on our behalf. When we feel overwhelmed, we're in good hands.

Ponder

What aspect of God's character means the most to you today, and why?

Pray

God, hold me in your strong but gentle hands.

"Leave it all in the Hands
that were wounded for you."

ELISABETH ELLIOT,
Keep a Quiet Heart

Morning Joy

Weeping may last through the night,
but joy comes with the morning.

PSALM 30:5 NLT

Pause

Do you wish you could wake up after a good night's sleep to find your situation nicely resolved? Oh, that life could be so predictable, right? Unfortunately, it doesn't work that way. The psalmist assures us that sorrow will end in the morning, but he doesn't specify which one. In fact, perhaps his reference to morning isn't calendar-related at all.

Consider this: perhaps "night" refers to the midnight hour of the soul. We can see neither anything good about our circumstances nor a way through them. Mystery shrouds our understanding until one day God breaks through the darkness with the light of truth and leads us to a place of discovery. We begin to see the ways in which he's been faithful. We catch a glimpse of his working behind the scenes. We begin to understand his sovereignty over our situation and his purposes for our pain.

The dawn of a new perspective brings joy. It pushes back the darkness and allows the Son to radiate his glory to us, in us, and through us.

Ponder

What spiritual truth helps to bring a new perspective about your circumstances?

Pray

Father, you know my thoughts, questions, and doubts. I invite you to banish the darkness with your light. Bring on the morning joy!

> "When every prop is gone—all else but God—then He knows your heart cry is one of utter dependence upon Him. You can also experience the 'hardest place in life' as being the sweetest. It is there one makes a fresh discovery of God."
>
> MRS. CHARLES E. COWMAN,
> *Streams in the Desert Sampler*

Good Father

Let us then approach God's throne of grace with confidence, so that we may receive mercy and find grace to help us in our time of need.

HEBREWS 4:16

Pause

The story's told of a king who called a meeting with his advisors. In the middle of their discussion, he noticed his daughter peering through the door, which was ajar. Without a moment's hesitation, he opened his arms and she came running. Such is the welcome our heavenly Father extends to us.

We might hesitate to approach him if we believe he doesn't really care about our concerns or that they're too trivial for him to take notice. Our pain might seem paltry to someone who deals with global pandemics, wars, and famine, right? Wrong. Nothing's further from the truth.

God cares deeply about what concerns me and you, and he invites us to come to his throne room anytime day or night. We needn't fear interrupting him. No matter what our need is, he promises to extend mercy and favor to help us through it.

Go ahead—run to him today. He can hardly wait to hold you.

Ponder

Do you feel free to approach God at any time? If not, why?

Pray

Father, help me picture you with arms open waiting for me to run into them.

"That's the way it is with our Father in Heaven. When you became a son or a daughter, when you were adopted into His family, He opened up for you through His Son's death on the cross a way of fellowship and relationship that makes it possible for you to bypass the temple and its animal sacrifices. You don't have to talk to God through a priest. You can go right into the presence of God Almighty and He will hear you."

DAVID JEREMIAH, *Prayer, the Great Adventure*

111

Finding Joy

Dear brothers and sisters, when troubles of any kind come your way, consider it an opportunity for great joy. For you know that when your faith is tested, your endurance has a chance to grow.

JAMES 1:2–3 NLT

Pause

I didn't feel very joyful as I bummed my way up fifteen stairs to my bedroom with a non-weight-bearing cast encasing my left leg. Twelve hours prior, I'd read James 1:2–3 and agreed with the writer's encouragement to view troubles as opportunities for joy. How was I to know that I'd rupture an Achilles tendon before day's end?

Throughout the next three months, I learned to apply the theology to which I'd so readily agreed. I found joy in experiencing supernatural strength to meet book deadlines, in friends bringing meals, and in my family's care. Even more, I found joy in developing stamina in the face of hardship and in learning to view each day, despite its challenges, as a gift to be enjoyed rather than a problem to be endured.

Choosing joy didn't change my circumstances, but it changed me and my attitude toward them. It's amazing what happens when we put spiritual principles into practice!

Ponder

Identify one reason for joy in your current challenge.

Pray

Lord, create in me a heart that regards my circumstances as an opportunity for joy.

"Joy is the settled assurance that God is in control of all the details of my life, the quiet confidence that ultimately everything is going to be all right, and the determined choice to praise God in all things."

KAY WARREN,
Choose Joy: Because Happiness Isn't Enough

Tug-of-War Prayer

*Now my soul is deeply troubled. Should I pray,
"Father, save me from this hour"? But this is the very
reason I came! Father, bring glory to your name.*

JOHN 12:27–28 NLT

Pause

Living at a year-round Christian camp provided opportunity to watch children play a variety of games. Tug-of-war was a classic. Back and forth, back and forth the teams pulled until the stronger won.

Have you ever played spiritual tug-of-war? It happens when our desires pull in opposite directions. Even Jesus dealt with it. Understandably, he wanted to avoid the suffering that awaited him. He considered praying that God would save him from it. At the same time, he knew that suffering was his purpose for coming, so he prayed instead that it would bring glory to God's name.

Jesus understands when we feel pulled in two directions. We want our crisis to end because suffering hurts. At the same time, we want God's will to be done even if that means our pain continues. We'll always be on the winning team if we pray for God to be honored.

Ponder

How might your thoughts in this situation be playing tug-of-war with God?

Pray

Father, grant me a heart that desires your glory above all else.

"Prayer is not telling God what to do. Prayer is partnering with God to see that His will is done. You don't have to fully understand what God's will is in order to pray that His will be done."

STORMIE OMARTIAN,
The Power of Praying for Your Adult Children

Life Saver

Trust in the LORD with all your heart and lean not on your own understanding; in all your ways submit to him, and he will make your paths straight.

PROVERBS 3:5–6

Pause

A piece of rescue equipment called a Lifesling hangs on a rail near the stern of our sailboat. Its storage case features diagrams and instructions that show us how to use it correctly if—heaven forbid—someone falls overboard when we're navigating open water.

I wish every crisis would come with diagrams and step-by-step instructions telling us how to survive when drowning feels like a very real possibility. It would sure make life easier.

Unfortunately, that's never going to happen, but we can hold on to hope when winds blow and waves slosh over us because God has given us his words as our Lifesling. They tell stories about how others have survived tumultuous times. When we feel like we're about to drown, his promises steady us. Reminders of his presence secure us. Reassurances of his power strengthen us. The waves batter us but they cannot sink us. His truth buoys us when we cling to it, and we are safe.

Ponder

What promise from God's Word is buoying you today?

Pray

God, thank you for giving me everything I need to survive this experience.

"We like to control the map of our life and know everything well in advance. But faith is content just knowing that God's promise cannot fail. This, in fact, is the excitement of walking with God."

JIM CYMBALA,
Fresh Faith: What Happens When Real Faith Ignites God's People

One Voice

Whether you turn to the right or to the left,
your ears will hear a voice behind you, saying,
"This is the way; walk in it."

ISAIAH 30:21

Pause

People wasted no time offering unsolicited advice when Job fell into a crisis. His wife told him to curse God and die, and his friends tried to convince him that God was punishing him. They meant well, in a warped way. Thankfully, Job knew enough not to listen.

I encountered a similar situation when leadership issues created an unhealthy culture in a ministry I was involved in. A trusted friend said, "Quit. Just walk away." I was tempted, but I prayed and listened for God's voice. He said, "Stay."

People generally want to help when they see someone in trouble, but caution is prudent. Our primary counsel comes from the Lord. He alone sees the bigger picture and he promises to give wisdom in abundance (James 1:5). When we don't know which way to turn, he'll tell us. He might speak through a godly friend or lead through circumstances. He may direct through impressions he puts in our heart. One thing's sure—the counsel he gives is always good.

Ponder

What is God's voice saying about your situation?

Pray

Lord, speak to me and tune my ear to hear your voice.

"Amid the thousands of shrill voices screaming for our attention, there is but one Voice we need to hear. The voice of the Lord Jesus Christ."

DAVID JEREMIAH,
Until Christ Returns: Living Faithfully Today While We Wait for Our Glorious Tomorrow

To-Do List

Rejoice always, pray continually,
give thanks in all circumstances;
for this is God's will for you in Christ Jesus.

1 THESSALONIANS 5:16–18

Pause

I'm a list-maker. At the end of my workday, I draw a line through the tasks I completed and then write a new list for the next morning. Sometimes the same items show up day after day. Those are usually the unpleasant chores I'd rather avoid.

The apostle Paul wrote a to-do list for Christ's followers. He penned three actions we're to take at all times no matter what circumstances we face—rejoice, pray, and give thanks. His intent is not to say we *must* do these things. Rather, it's that we *can* do these things because it's God's will and he'll help us.

Choosing joy, conversing with God throughout the day, and expressing gratitude show up on a believer's to-do list every day not because they're unpleasant chores we'd rather avoid but because they're good for us. Doing them releases hormones that contribute to our feelings of contentment and pleasure. Because God designed us, he knows what's best for us and will help us do these things.

Ponder

Add "rejoice always, pray continually, give thanks in all circumstances" to your to-do list.

Pray

Father, thank you for telling me what to do and then helping me do it.

"God never asks us to do anything or go through anything that He will not empower us to do or give us the grace to endure."

PATSY BURNETTE,
The Heart That Heals: Healing Our Brokenness Through the Promises of God

Thankful

*Enter his gates with thanksgiving and his courts with
praise; give thanks to him and praise his name.
For the LORD is good and his love endures forever;
his faithfulness continues through all generations.*

PSALM 100:4–5

Pause

It was our first winter living on a boat. Temperatures dropped below freezing and ice formed on the river. It floated by, thudding and scraping our hull. Visions of the Titanic floated in my head. Then our furnace died and temperatures plunged indoors, too. The local expert repair guy promised to come but didn't show. He promised again. And again. We waited and shivered for two weeks.

Knowing God led us to this boat-home helped keep me from despair. So did intentionally giving thanks. While I wasn't thankful for frigid temperatures and repair costs, I expressed gratitude for God's presence, winter's beauty, and safety on slippery docks.

Giving thanks in hard places doesn't come naturally. The key lies in surrendering our wills and expectations to the Lord. It's an outer demonstration of an inner choice to trust him with our fears and frustrations. We bless him, and he blesses us with calm.

Ponder

Finish the sentence: "Today I am thankful for _____."

Pray

Father, I give you my fears and frustrations. And I give you thanks for loving me.

"I have learned that in every circumstance that comes my way, I can choose to respond in one of two ways: I can whine or I can worship! And I can't worship without giving thanks. It just isn't possible. When we choose the pathway of worship and giving thanks, especially in the midst of difficult circumstances, there is a fragrance, a radiance, that issues forth out of our lives to bless the Lord and others."

NANCY LEIGH DEMOSS,
Choosing Gratitude: Your Journey to Joy

Shadows

Even though I walk through the darkest valley,
I will fear no evil, for you are with me;
your rod and your staff, they comfort me.

PSALM 23:4

Pause

The road to my in-laws' home wound through the woods. Towering evergreens blocked sun by day and moon by night. My father-in-law was in his late eighties when he began having second thoughts about driving that road, especially at night. Darkness was one thing, but his dimming eyesight added to his doubts. His eyes played tricks on him, he said. He saw shapes in the shadows, and he couldn't tell whether they were real or imaginary. The stress wasn't worth it.

Darkness can play tricks on us, too, when crisis strikes and we don't understand what's happening. We see a "what-if" lurking in the shadows, and our minds tell us it's real. That's when stress and fear kick in. What to do?

Invite Jesus to take your hand and walk through the darkness with you. His presence will shed light on your path. His light will expose the hidden "what-ifs" and remove your fears.

Ponder

Identify the "what-ifs" lurking in the shadows of your mind.

Pray

God, shine the light of truth into my mind so darkness cannot control my imagination.

> "Darkness does something to a place, doesn't it?
> It distorts. It becomes a canvas for the imagination.
> The good news is that shadows are only the
> deflection of light. They can frighten,
> but they can do no harm."

DAVID JEREMIAH,
What Are You Afraid Of?

Endless Supply

Because of the LORD's great love we are not consumed,
for his compassions never fail. They are new every
morning; great is your faithfulness.

LAMENTATIONS 3:22–23

Pause

The coronavirus trapped people into panic buying. Like a plague of locusts descending and stripping vegetation bare, so the population flocked into grocery stores and stripped the shelves. I was in Alberta visiting my mother when the World Health Organization declared the virus a pandemic. By the time I returned home several days later, my favorite grocery store was nearly empty. Flour? None. Sugar? Nada. Fresh meat, butter, cheese, milk, peanut butter, beans, rice, pasta—*vanished*. The sight felt surreal.

As angst began rising in me, the Holy Spirit brought Lamentations 3:22–23 to mind. He reminded me that God's supplies never run short. His storehouse of compassion is always full. His faithfulness is available in abundance. We never have to wonder whether we'll exhaust his love. There's enough to cover our needs and more. Day after day after day, he knows our needs and meets them because of who he is. He is God, we are his children, and we have no need to panic.

Ponder

What do you need most from God's storehouse today?

Pray

Father, thank you for promising to meet my needs according to your glorious riches.

"God loves each of us as if there were only one of us to love."

AUGUSTINE (AD 354–439),
bishop of Hippo

127

Fighting Our Giants

David said to the Philistine, "You come against me with sword and spear and javelin, but I come against you in the name of the LORD Almighty, the God of the armies of Israel, whom you have defied."

1 SAMUEL 17:45

Pause

Goliath towered over the teenager David and scoffed, "If you think you can take me down, then think again!" His intimidation tactics didn't work.

David stood his ground. He acknowledged the giant's weaponry meant to destroy him, but then he revealed his battle strategy. He would fight in the name of God Almighty, and he would win.

We all face personal giants. A crisis towers over us and intimidates us. It threatens to destroy our marriage and family, our health and livelihood, our sanity, future, and hope. It sends shock waves through us. But we can stand our ground.

We don't fight our Goliath in our own strength. We use spiritual weaponry. We're soldiers in the army of the Lord Almighty, so we call on his name to help us. We will neither retreat nor surrender. Victory is ours regardless of what the giant says.

Ponder

What is your giant telling you? How is he trying to intimidate you?

Pray

God of heavenly armies, take down my giant in the power of your name.

"[Satan] vies for the bedside position,
hoping to be the first voice you hear.
He covets your waking thoughts, those early,
pillow-born emotions. He awakes you with words
of worry, stirs you with thoughts of stress.
If you dread the day before you begin your day,
mark it down: your giant has been by your bed."

MAX LUCADO, *Facing Your Giants: A David and Goliath Story for Everyday People*

The Gift of Peace

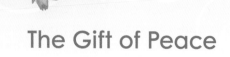

I am leaving you with a gift—peace of mind and heart. And the peace I give is a gift the world cannot give. So don't be troubled or afraid.

JOHN 14:27 NLT

Pause

For his sixty-fourth birthday, I gave my husband two hours of hands-on training with a marine diesel mechanic. My husband wanted to better understand how our sailboat engine operates, so this seemed the ideal present. The training equipped him for the best possible outcome should our engine fail while we're on an excursion. I had no doubt that he would accept this gift because he needed and wanted it.

Jesus offers a gift of peace to us because he knows we need and want it even more than we realize this for ourselves. It's ideal for us. It steadies us when our path feels rough and long. It guards us from fear and despair should that path take an unwelcome detour.

Let's not hesitate to accept this gift. We access it by training our minds on the truth of who God is and focusing on his character. The better we understand who he is, the more peace we experience. The peace he gives is the gift that keeps on giving.

Ponder

What aspect of God's character brings peace to your heart today?

Pray

Lord, thank you for this gift of peace. It's perfect!

"Those who are in the best of circumstances but without God can never find peace, but those in the worst of circumstances but with God need never lack peace."

JOHN MACARTHUR,
MacArthur New Testament Commentary

Jesus Prays for You

Who then will condemn us? No one—
for Christ Jesus died for us and was raised to life for us,
and he is sitting in the place of honor
at God's right hand, pleading for us.

ROMANS 8:34 NLT

Pause

Two months into the pandemic lockdown, I wrote a newsletter to subscribers in which I was really honest about my emotional state. I'd done well until then, but one day a wave of sadness caught me off guard. I grieved for so many losses felt by so many people, myself included. Physical exhaustion after helping my daughter and her husband make a difficult move and the pain of a cracked tailbone compounded my state of mind.

To my surprise, readers emailed me with assurances of their prayers. Most of them were strangers. I felt so blessed. Knowing they were interceding for me filled me with hope.

A far greater measure of hope fills me when I think that Jesus prays for us. We don't even need to tell him our heart's silent cries; he already knows. No matter what pain we're going through, he intercedes according to the Father's will. He's got our backs 24/7. We are indeed blessed.

Ponder

What is your greatest prayer concern today?

Pray

Jesus, thank you for knowing my greatest prayer concern even if I don't voice it.

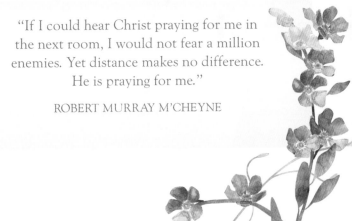

"If I could hear Christ praying for me in the next room, I would not fear a million enemies. Yet distance makes no difference. He is praying for me."

ROBERT MURRAY M'CHEYNE

133

Undefeatable

There is a river whose streams make glad the city of
God, the holy place where the Most High dwells.
God is within her, she will not fall;
God will help her at break of day.

PSALM 46:4–5

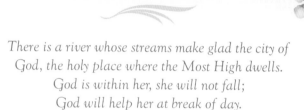

Several years ago, I faced a health crisis that transformed the way I think about my body. I began to understand it as the temple of God (1 Corinthians 3:16). It's an amazing truth. Whereas the Lord once dwelt in a temple built by human hands, he now lives in his people.

Imagine! This God is master over the impossible. His power brought the entire universe into existence and holds it in place. His power split the Red Sea and raised Christ from the dead. And this God makes his home in us.

Because God lives in us, nothing can overcome us. He is our refuge, our strength, our very-present help in times of trouble. Everything we need to conquer doubt, despair, and defeat is at our disposal because all-powerful God dwells in us.

We needn't fear hardships. They cannot destroy us. God's mighty power works in us, and we will not fall.

Ponder

Think about other biblical accounts that show God's mighty power.

Pray

Father, astound me with demonstrations of your power working on my behalf in this situation.

"If it's true that the Spirit of God dwells in us and that our bodies are the Holy Spirit's temple, then shouldn't there be a huge difference between the person who has the Spirit of God living inside of him or her and the person who does not?"

FRANCIS CHAN, *Forgotten God: Reversing Our Tragic Neglect of the Holy Spirit*

This Day

The LORD is good,
A strength and stronghold in the day of trouble;
He knows [He recognizes, cares for, and understands
fully] those who take refuge and trust in Him.

NAHUM 1:7 AMP

Pause

The border closure between the United States and Canada
during the pandemic separated us from our daughter and
her husband. They bought their first home during that time.
We hoped to help them move, but we saw no signs that
the border would open. We all wondered, "How long is
this going to last?"

Maybe you're wondering the same thing. Know that this
day of trouble is exactly that—a day. Every day ends at
exactly the right time. Don't fret about the past or worry
about the future. Keep your focus on today. Look for
evidences of God's presence and goodness. Trust him
to be your strength until he brings the sun to set on your
situation.

God knows where you are and everything about you. He knows your tears, your fears, desires, and concerns. You're on his mind and in his heart today, all day, every day.

Ponder

The day of trouble is only a day and will end when God ordains. In the meantime, think of some evidence of God's presence you've witnessed today.

Pray

Lord, thank you for caring for me through this day that seems endless.

"God is the God of 'right now.'
He doesn't want you sitting around regretting yesterday. Nor does He want you wringing your hands and worrying about the future.
He wants you focusing on what He is saying to you and putting in front of you ... right now."

PRISCILLA SHIRER, *Discerning the Voice of God:
How to Recognize When He Speaks*

Healed from Shame

Then I acknowledged my sin to you and did not cover up my iniquity. I said, "I will confess my transgressions to the LORD." And you forgave the guilt of my sin.

PSALM 32:5

Pause

My friend Mary Ross Ward was fortyish and suffering from medical issues that baffled her doctors. In desperation, she saw a nurse practitioner who practiced standard medicine with a holistic bent. That appointment set her on a new course.

For years, Mary had lived with hidden shame from poor choices she'd made as a young woman. She knew God had forgiven her, but she could not forgive herself. The guilt she carried nearly destroyed her body. Hope came and healing followed as she began to understand that Christ's death also erased her guilt.

King David hit a similar crisis of body and soul when hiding his adulterous affair (Psalm 32:3–5). Secrecy and shame sapped his strength and led to despair, but walking in the truth of God's love and forgiveness set him free.

Can you relate to these stories? If so, release your guilt to God. He longs to bring healing to the hidden places in your heart.

Ponder

Reflect on the truth that Jesus took your guilt to the cross. You are free!

Pray

Lord, thank you for erasing my guilt and taking my shame.

"God's love endures forever.
You are not too broken for God to fix.
You are not too dirty for God to cleanse.
You are not too far for God to reach.
You are not too guilty for God to forgive.
You are not too worthless for God to love.
God loves you right where you are."

RASHAWN COPELAND,
*Start Where You Are: How God Meets You in Your Mess,
Loves You Through It, and Leads You Out of It*

Refresh

I pray that from his glorious, unlimited resources he will empower you with inner strength through his Spirit. Then Christ will make his home in your hearts as you trust in him. Your roots will grow down into God's love and keep you strong.

EPHESIANS 3:16–17 NLT

Pause

I own four planters and fill each with a variety of annuals that I buy locally. Because I live in an area with limited shopping options, sometimes the only plants available look exhausted. Their blooms droop and their leaves hang limp. I transplant them into fresh soil and fertilizer, and then I give them a long, cool drink. Tender loving care transforms them into healthy flowering plants that beautify our dock.

Have difficult circumstances left you feeling like my poor plants look when I buy them? Exhausted. Droopy. Limp. Does your soul feel dry and thirsty for refreshment? If so, it's necessary and good to press pause and bask in God's tender care. Sit in his presence with no agenda other than to be with him. You might only have the luxury of doing so for a few minutes, but that's okay. Spending a few minutes in quiet with him will empower and strengthen you. You will flourish again.

Ponder

Sit in silence and imagine God holding you close to his heart.

Pray

Father, I'm weary. Please pour your love and Spirit over me.

"The only hope we have is daily dependence on the living Lord. It's the only way we can make it. He's touched with our feelings of infirmity, our weaknesses, our inability in the dark and lonely times to say no. He's touched with that. And He says, 'I'm ready with all the power you need. Call on Me and I'll give you what you need.'"

CHARLES R. SWINDOLL,
Bedtime Blessings

No Separation

Who shall separate us from the love of Christ?
Shall trouble or hardship or persecution or famine
or nakedness or danger or sword?...
No, in all these things we are more than
conquerors through him who loved us.

ROMANS 8:35, 37

Pause

The pandemic taught us a new term: social distancing. As much as possible, we kept a six-foot space between ourselves and others when shopping, standing in lines, going for walks, and speaking with neighbors. Hugs, handshakes, and high-fives were a no-go. Travel restrictions and border closures separated friends and family for months.

Not being able to visit my kids and grandkids made my heart ache. Facebook posts showed pictures of grandparents visiting their littles through closed windows, but mine lived hours away. I felt sadness, but it didn't compare to the sorrow others felt when they couldn't sit at the bedsides of their sick loved ones.

Hardships can separate us from those we love, but they can never separate us from the God who loves us. Rather than distancing himself from us when we need him, he makes himself readily available. He's our "ever-present help in trouble" whatever that trouble looks like (Psalm 46:1).

Ponder

Complete this sentence: "God's love surrounds me while I'm in the midst of _____."

Pray

Lord, thank you that difficult circumstances can never restrict your presence with me.

"You can look forward with hope, because one day there will be no more separation, no more scars, and no more suffering in My Father's House. It's the home of your dreams!"

ANNE GRAHAM LOTZ,
Heaven: My Father's House

Deeply Loved

You keep track of all my sorrows.
You have collected all my tears in your bottle.
You have recorded each one in your book.

PSALM 56:8 NLT

Pause

The song, "Jesus Loves Me," was a childhood favorite, and I still enjoy it. Its simplicity calms my fear: "Jesus loves me, this I know, for the Bible tells me so …"

Having experienced several crises in my sixty-some years, I understand a few gems about God's love. While I cannot begin to grasp its depth, I know it's not a general, sweeping brushstroke of concern for the planet's population. It's not a one-size-fits-every-heart. His love for you and me is intimate and custom designed for our personality and needs.

God's love is so personal that he's aware of every tear we cry, even those we stifle. There's no sorrow or disappointment we can hide from him, nor should we try.

He knows our hurts and our pain, and he wants us to trust him with those things.

Is sorrow weighing you down? Tell God how you feel. He wants you to talk with him. He desires your presence and trust. Confide in him, my friend. His love for you runs deeper than words can express.

Ponder

Reflect on the simple yet profound truth that God loves you intimately.

Pray

Father, thank you for letting me cry on your strong shoulder.

"God's love isn't based on me.
It's simply placed on me. And it's the place
from which I should live … loved."

LYSA TERKEURST,
*Uninvited: Living Loved When You Feel Less Than,
Left Out, and Lonely*

Mountain-Maker

I lift up my eyes to the mountains—
where does my help come from?
My help comes from the LORD,
the Maker of heaven and earth.

PSALM 121:1–2

Pause

British Columbia is my home. Every time I fly north or east, I cross the Canadian Rockies. They're stunning, especially in winter when snow covers their peaks. And when the sun rises or sets on them—oh my—words cannot describe their beauty.

When we lived in Nepal, I saw Mt. Everest from the air. At 29,029 feet, it stands more than twice the height of the tallest mountain in the Rockies. Its sight left me in awe. But here's something that amazes me more.

The God who spoke these mountains into existence stoops to listen to our cries (Psalm 116:2). When trouble comes our way, we needn't worry about how we'll make our way through it. One glimpse at the towering peaks assures us that his strength is more than sufficient to fight our battles. Like the children's song says, my God is so big, so strong, and so mighty, there's nothing my God cannot do—for you!

Ponder

The Mountain-Maker cherishes you. What difference does this truth make to you?

Pray

God, you spoke mountains into existence. You can surely speak hope into my heart today.

> "Living becomes an awesome business when you realize that you spend every moment of your life in the sight and company of an omniscient, omnipresent Creator."

J. I. PACKER,
Knowing God

Choosing Joy

Even though the fig trees have no blossoms, and there are no grapes on the vines; even though the olive crop fails, and the fields lie empty and barren; even though the flocks die in the fields, and the cattle barns are empty, yet I will rejoice in the LORD! I will be joyful in the God of my salvation!

HABAKKUK 3:17–18 NLT

Pause

My maternal grandmother was born in Russia. Her father was murdered when she was about ten years old, so she supported her family by chasing crows from sunflower fields. She received crusty bread rolls in return.

Grandma knew poverty well into her adulthood, but she also knew God. Faith in him gave her strength and perseverance through decades of hardship after immigrating to Canada. Her attitude reminds me of the prophet Habakkuk, who clung to hope even in utter desolation.

How easily Habakkuk could have slipped into a negative, fearful perspective, but he didn't. Neither did he shift into a power-of-positive-thinking mentality. He acknowledged the difficulties and then chose to rejoice in the Lord. He knew that crisis upon crisis could not diminish God's power or change his nature. Circumstances looked dismal, but they couldn't dampen his hope.

Ponder

In what aspect of God's nature can you rejoice today?

Pray

Lord, even though my situation appears hopeless and I don't understand what's happening or why, I will rejoice in you.

> "Practicing defiant joy is the declaration that the darkness does not and will not win. When we fight back with joy, we embrace a reality that is more real than what we're enduring and we awaken to the deepest reality of our identity as beloved, joyful children of God."
>
> MARGARET FEINBERG, *Fight Back With Joy: Celebrate More. Regret Less. Stare Down Your Greatest Fears*

Comfort Others

Praise be to the God and Father of our Lord Jesus Christ, the Father of compassion and the God of all comfort, who comforts us in all our troubles, so that we can comfort those in any trouble with the comfort we ourselves receive from God.

2 CORINTHIANS 1:3–4

Pause

After our infant daughter underwent brain surgery, she shared a hospital room with a boy the same age. His mother and I visited while we sat by our babies' bedsides. She expressed fear for her son's life, so I offered to pray for him. That opened a conversation about Christ and the hope he gives us in crisis.

God never wastes our pain. He uses it to deepen and mature us, but he also uses it to reveal his comfort so that we might, in turn, comfort others in trouble. In the context of 2 Corinthians 1, the original word for comfort is *paraklesis*. This means more than offering sympathy. It implies "making strong or brave."

No doubt, God will bring someone into your life who feels hopeless in her crisis. Be that person who comes alongside and offers the strength and courage you've received in yours.

Ponder

What words or act of comfort can you extend to someone today?

Pray

Father, open my eyes to someone who needs comfort today.

"You are able to provide comfort only when you have been through the fire. Only because you've been in the furnace of affliction. Only because you've suffered loss. Only because you know the depth of hurt and pain. Only because you know what loneliness, emptiness, uncertainty, and fear are all about. Then you will be ready to comfort others."

CHARLES STANLEY, *God Is in Control: An Unshakable Peace in the Midst of Life's Storms*

Rest

He came to a broom bush, sat down under it
and prayed that he might die.
"I have had enough, LORD," he said.
"Take my life; I am no better than my ancestors."
Then he lay down under the bush and fell asleep.

1 KINGS 19:4–5

Pause

Elijah had witnessed God prove his power over Baal. Then he defeated and killed four hundred and fifty false prophets. After that, he prophesied rain and it fell for the first time in three years. Finally, he outran King Ahab's chariot to Jezreel. That's when he heard about Queen Jezebel wanting him dead.

Jezebel's threat overrode the truth Elijah knew and had just witnessed. It plunged him from the spiritual mountaintop to a pit of despair in a nanosecond. Do you think physical exhaustion played a role? I do.

Extreme fatigue can make us vulnerable to wrong thinking. We exchange the truth for a false reality that skews our perspective. Therefore, rest is essential when we're in crisis mode. Sleep can be difficult, but do what you must to care for yourself. A good rest helps keep us in the right frame of mind.

Ponder

Rest for a few minutes. Close your eyes and enjoy—guilt-free.

Pray

Father, provide the opportunity and ability for me to sleep deeply.

"In place of our exhaustion and physical fatigue, He will give us rest. All He asks is that we come to Him … that we spend a while thinking about Him, meditating on Him, talking to Him, listening in silence, occupying ourselves with Him—totally and thoroughly lost in the hiding place of His presence."

CHARLES R. SWINDOLL,
Growing Strong in the Seasons of Life

Praying God's Promises

Remember your word to your servant, for you have given me hope. My comfort in my suffering is this: Your promise preserves my life.

PSALM 119:49–50

Pause

Gene and I faced a family relationship crisis that hurt deeply. There was so much we didn't understand. We felt like we were looking at a jigsaw puzzle with half the pieces missing. I cried, we prayed, and then we prayed some more. We reminded God of his own words: "You said you give wisdom to those who ask. We're asking, so please give it to us. You said you're close to the brokenhearted, so please come near to us."

We were cautious not to take God's promises out of context. Neither did we consider praying them like one might rub a magic genie lamp—remind God of his promises and presto! Rather, we saw his word as his bond to us; therefore, we could hold him to it.

We reminded God of his promises, and he reminded us of his love for us. He didn't answer with immediate reconciliation, but he comforted us and gave us patience in the wait.

Ponder

Which of God's promises can you pray today?

Pray

Lord, thank you for your promise to hear my cries. I know you're listening.

"Every promise of Scripture is a writing of God, which may be pleaded before him with this reasonable request, 'Do as thou has said.' The Creator will not cheat his creature who depends upon his truth; and, far more, the heavenly Father will not break his word to his own child."

CHARLES SPURGEON

Trading Worry for Songs in the Night

On my bed I remember you; I think of you through the watches of the night. Because you are my help, I sing in the shadow of your wings.

PSALM 63:6–7

Pause

Worry knows how to keep me awake at night. Unless I restrain my thoughts, they ricochet from one what-if to another. *What if the economy collapses? What if our kids make choices that hurt them in the end? What if my husband dies before me?* I ask myself random questions and then come up with potential outcomes based solely on my imagination. Can you relate?

Allowing nighttime thoughts to run rampant never goes well for me, so I appreciate the psalmist's testimony. When sleep evaded him, he meditated on God's character. He pondered the ways in which God had helped him. He visualized God's protection over him.

Worry and worship are mutually exclusive. Anxiety multiplies when we entertain what-ifs and unknowns. But meditating on God's faithfulness, patience, wisdom, and sovereignty settles our minds and soothes our souls. Practicing this discipline calms even the most anxious heart. It chases worry away and turns sleeplessness into songs of joy.

Ponder

How would you describe the thoughts you think when you can't sleep?

Pray

Father, please help me focus my thoughts on you in the night.

"That thing you can't stop worrying about?
Verbally give it over to the Lord. Say out loud,
'God, this is hard for me. I feel like I have more
control if I keep worrying about (insert worry).
But I fully give this to You. I trust You.
You are good and You are good at being God.'"

LYSA TERKEURST

Wait

I wait for the LORD, my whole being waits, and in his word I put my hope. I wait for the Lord more than watchmen wait for the morning, more than watchmen wait for the morning.

PSALM 130:5–6

Pause

Abram and Sarai waited more than two decades for the son God promised. Sarai was already past menopause when the promise came. Perhaps she feared she'd die before God could work his miracle. Either impatience or panic influenced her decision to give him a hand. Rushing ahead of his timing created chaos in her home and made her a bitter woman.

Waiting on God means waiting for the right time, and only he knows when that time has come. It's learning to dance in his rhythm and follow his lead. It never goes well if we take that lead from him.

While we wait, God works in us and behind the scenes, choreographing the details. Let's be patient. Let's hope in his promise to help us persevere more than we hope for a particular outcome. The night watchmen fulfill their role knowing with certainty that the dawn will come. With the same certainty, we know God will come through for us.

Ponder

What lessons are you learning as you wait for God to act?

Pray

Father, help me trust your lead. I don't want to step on your toes.

"When you find yourself sinking in the quicksand, there is little else you can do but cry to the Lord. Sometimes He allows the 'quicksand' experiences to turn you to Him. Wait for God. Acknowledge that He is in control. Give Him the pieces of your broken heart and watch Him work for you. You can depend on His faithfulness."

WARREN W. WIERSBE, *Prayer, Praise & Promises: A Daily Walk Through the Psalms*

Moving Beyond Dismay

Be gracious to me, O LORD, for I am pining away;
Heal me, O LORD, for my bones are dismayed.

PSALM 6:2 NASB

Pause

In Hebrew, the word *dismay* implies collapsing in a heap after receiving bad news or losing hope in difficult circumstances.

Insomnia struck after leg injuries left me in a wheelchair. Physical and emotional energy seeped away, and my thoughts spiraled down, down, down into dismay. I began to fear never regaining my strength or sleeping well again.

Things changed when I recognized the connection between my thoughts and despair. I began retraining my mind to focus on God's promises, such as those found in Isaiah 50:7: "Because the Sovereign LORD helps me, I will not be disgraced. Therefore have I set my face like flint, and I know I will not be put to shame." The living God, for whom nothing is impossible, is our helper. He's bigger than any hardship we face. He hears our cries. He's on our side. And He's *by* our side.

How are you really doing today? If you're feeling dismayed, then reread the preceding paragraph. Make it your focus and prayer: "God, you've promised to help me. You're bigger than my hardship, you hear my cries, you're on my side, and you're by my side. Thank you."

Ponder

What part of Isaiah 50:7 means the most to you? Why?

Pray

Father, be gracious to me. Rescue me from dismay as I focus on your promises.

> "Wide awake to the presence of God, I realized I had been so focused on asking why a good God allowed bad things to happen that I was missing out on the nearness of God all along. In becoming preoccupied with the why, I was missing the who."

MARGARET FEINBERG,
Wonderstruck: Awaken to the Nearness of God

Snuggle

*Even if my father and mother abandon me,
the L*ORD *will hold me close.*

PSALM 27:10 NLT

Pause

I looked forward to visiting our youngest granddaughter, Lexi, for her first birthday. Four months had passed since I'd last seen her, and I wasn't sure whether she would remember me. I needn't have worried. The moment I picked her up, she laid her head on my shoulder, snuggled, and smiled. Lexi did my "grandma heart" good.

I will cherish that sweet moment with Lexi forever. Perhaps that's how our heavenly Father feels if we nestle into him when we're in trouble. We might feel frantic or afraid. We might try to escape the pain. We might try to wrestle control from his hands. That's our natural response if we don't believe he's trustworthy.

But if God is who he says he is, then he is completely trustworthy. He always has our best interest in mind and promises to be faithful. He accepts, guides, and protects us. He wants to hold us close, but he lets us choose.

Go ahead—rest your head on his shoulder and snuggle. Do his "father heart" good.

Ponder

Imagine God wrapping his gentle, strong arms around you. Relax. Smile.

Pray

Father, help me learn to nestle, not wrestle, when you hold me.

"Snuggle in God's arms. When you are hurting, when you feel lonely, left out.
Let Him cradle you, comfort you, reassure you of His all-sufficient power and love."

KAY ARTHUR,
My Savior, My Friend: A Daily Devotional

Tie a Knot and Hang On

My soul clings to You;
Your right hand upholds me.

PSALM 63:8 NASB

Pause

One of my favorite wall posters in younger years showed a kitten clutching the end of a knotted rope. The text said, "When all else fails, tie a knot and hang on."

We all reach the end of our rope sooner or later. I reached mine during one whopper of a year. It started in January with leg injuries that left me in a wheelchair until mid-April. Two weeks after I began walking again, my body broke into shingles. I'd barely recovered when my youngest daughter decided to marry within five weeks, so I shifted into full-time planning. My son's wife delivered a baby prematurely a week after the wedding. Then my husband was diagnosed with prostate cancer and contracted a blood infection. I tied a big, big faith knot and hung on to the Lord.

To what do you cling when life delivers blow after blow? Do you hang onto something that gives false hope, or do you cling to God and his promises? Anything other than the Lord will let us down, but he holds us securely and keeps us from falling.

Ponder

What or who do you tie your knot to when all else fails?

Pray

Father, I place my hope in you alone. Hold me close as I cling to you.

"The point of wrestling with God is to give you an opportunity to cling to him. God wants you to hang on to him no matter what—and the result will be blessing. ... In that divine wrestling match, you may feel wounded, but you will also receive a blessing you couldn't have received any other way."

JENNIFER ROTHSCHILD, *God Is Just Not Fair: Finding Hope When Life Doesn't Make Sense*

God's Reality

So we fix our eyes not on what is seen, but on what is unseen, since what is seen is temporary, but what is unseen is eternal.

2 CORINTHIANS 4:18

Pause

Barbara felt devastated. After being unemployed for eighteen months, her husband had been interviewed several times for a job at a good company. Things looked promising until Human Resources said that they were no longer considering him for the position and were looking elsewhere.

Barb saw a closed door, but she chose to fix her eyes on the unseen instead. She spoke 2 Corinthians 4:18 aloud and prayed, "I trust that you're working out your perfect will behind the scenes. What I see isn't the whole truth about our situation. I will keep trusting until I see your will become reality." Peace flooded her anxious heart. Days later, a company executive called, took her husband out to lunch and offered him the position!

Closed doors and impossibilities are not necessarily the whole truth. God may be doing something unseen and preparing to reveal a different reality. Learn to see life through eyes of faith. Keep trusting until his will becomes reality in your life.

Ponder

What are you fixing your eyes on—the seen or the unseen?

Pray

God, I believe you're working. Show me the full picture in your time.

"Regardless of what crisis or complexity may be threatening to engulf your life, God is at work. You may not see it, but you need to know it's true. And He's not just doing one or two or a few things in that situation. He is doing *a thousand* or more things."

NANCY DEMOSS WOLGEMUTH,
The Quiet Place: Daily Devotional Readings

Carried

*In all their suffering he also suffered, and he
personally rescued them. In his love and mercy
he redeemed them. He lifted them up and
carried them through all the years.*

ISAIAH 63:9 NLT

Pause

Watching my son carry his little ones warms my heart. Most
often they sit content in his arms, feeling secure and safe
from the world. They lay their heads on his shoulder when
they're tired or needing comfort. But it's not always so
serene. Sometimes they're upset, and he holds them to
help them gain composure.

This is the picture of God carrying us—his children—
especially when we're suffering. He hurts when we hurt,
and he scoops us into his arms to soothe us. Sometimes,
we snuggle close to the Lord to receive his comfort. Other
times, we wrestle against him because our pain makes
us angry. He feels with us in that emotion, too, and his

love compels him to hold us as we struggle through to a different perspective.

Our heavenly Father is always alert to our needs and cares deeply for our well-being. His arms are our safe place, and we can trust him to keep us there.

Ponder

Meditate on the truth that God's arms are your safe space.

Pray

Father, I'm reaching my arms out to you. Please carry me.

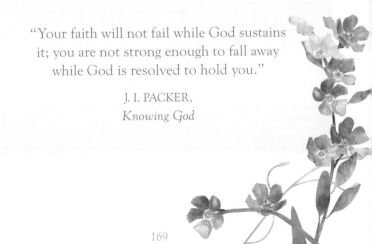

"Your faith will not fail while God sustains it; you are not strong enough to fall away while God is resolved to hold you."

J. I. PACKER,
Knowing God

Heart Care

My health may fail, and my spirit may grow weak,
but God remains the strength of my heart;
he is mine forever.

PSALM 73:26 NLT

Pause

Cynthia's brother-in-law needed a life-saving heart transplant. As he waited for a donor, she encouraged him by buying a Bible and highlighting every mention of the word *heart*. At a glance, he could see how much God cared for him.

God cares about every part of who we are—physical, mental, emotional, and spiritual. So, while Cynthia's brother-in-law was facing a physical crisis of the heart, God also cared about his "heart"—"the center of man's character—who he really is."*

The Bible mentions the heart in this context nearly a thousand times. A well-known verse says, "The LORD is

*Pastor Stephen Kyeyune, *Shaping the Society Christianity and Culture*

close to the brokenhearted and saves those who are crushed in spirit" (Psalm 34:18). He knows when we hurt. He understands our angst as we wait for healing to come. He is our strength when our hearts grow weak. And he is with us just as Cynthia and her family waited with her brother-in-law for the call that a donor heart had arrived.

Ponder

Where do you feel most weak today?

Pray

Father, thank you for being close to me in my broken-hearted state. You are my strength. You are mine.

"Our physical bodies fail us. Our emotions are sometimes as fragile as soap bubbles. But nothing about God is fragile. His embrace erases, encases, and replaces the deepest pain with a comfort unlike any other. He can massage a broken soul back to life like a surgeon would massage a still heart until it beats again ... if we place our heart in his hands."

CYNTHIA RUCHTI, author of *Afraid of the Light*

171

Guard Your Mind

The thief's purpose is to steal and kill and destroy.
My purpose is to give them a rich and satisfying life.

JOHN 10:10 NLT

Pause

I pulled into our driveway after running errands. A difficult conversation with a family member a month prior replayed in my head. I felt hurt and anger try to drag me into a dark place. Then a thought came to mind: *Do your family a favor. Drive away and never return.*

That's how Satan works. He attacks our minds (especially when we're vulnerable) because he knows that the thoughts we dwell on eventually become actions. Those actions determine our destiny, and his desire for our destiny is destruction.

God, on the other hand, wants an abundant life for us. Don't mistake that for an easy life. It's a life rich with peace, contentment, and hope. It's filled to the brim with joy that comes from intimacy with him.

Be alert to the thoughts that pop into your mind during this season. If they're not truth-based, then don't let them linger. Guard your mind with God's truth to ensure your destiny will be the one he desires.

Ponder

Identify a recent thought that's not truth-based. What *is* the truth?

Pray

Lord, make me aware of wrong thinking and help me focus on what's right.

"Most of life's battles are won
or lost in the mind."

CRAIG GROESCHEL,
Soul Detox: Clean Living in a Contaminated World

Our Strong Fortress

The LORD is my light and my salvation—
so why should I be afraid? The LORD is my fortress,
protecting me from danger, so why should I tremble?

PSALM 27:1 NLT

Pause

I've traveled to Eastern Europe numerous times for ministry purposes. On several occasions, I've had opportunity to visit ancient fortresses. These amazing structures were built strategically on hilltops to give residents a view of the surrounding territory. This enabled them to see enemies approaching and then prepare for battle. Even if enemies were able to make a sneak attack, the fortresses' thick stone walls would have prevented them easy access.

God identifies himself as our fortress. He invites us to run to him for safety from our enemies. Our difficult situation itself is not our foe, but fear is. It shoots a barrage of what-if arrows at our mind. Along with fear comes the enemy of doubt, and we question God's presence or care for us.

Making the Lord our fortress means we fill our minds with his promises. His words become our weapon and make us impenetrable. The enemies of fear and doubt will attack, but they cannot harm us.

Ponder

What enemies are trying to attack you in your situation?

Pray

Father, I take refuge in you. Be my fortress and my safe place.

"The name of the Lord ... is a fortified tower. ...
His name will never fail. His name will never be
defeated. His Name will never be reduced to rubble.
That's why His name instills confidence.
It is strong enough, 'mighty' (CEV) enough,
to provide 'a place of protection' (MSG)
for those who love Him."

LIZ CURTIS HIGGS

But God

Once you were not a people, but now you are
God's people; once you had not received mercy,
but now you have received mercy.

1 PETER 2:10 ESV

Pause

The Bible is filled with accounts that looked hopeless apart from God's intervention. The addition of two little words changed everything. Reading the following examples, can you guess what they are?

Joseph's brothers meant harm when they sold him into slavery, but God meant it for the good of an entire nation (Genesis 50:20). Saul hunted daily for David, but God didn't allow him to find David (1 Samuel 23:14). Laban cheated his son-in-law, Jacob, but God didn't let him cause bodily harm (Genesis 31:7). Here's one of my favorites: "You killed the author of life, but God raised him from the dead" (Acts 3:15).

"But God" puts a new spin on our circumstances. They might feel intimidating and look impossible, but he is able to create beauty from ashes and bring joy from our mourning. We're wounded but he heals us. We're brokenhearted but he restores us. Life can unravel in an instant and we have no idea how our story will end, but God has the final say.

Ponder

How does "but God" bring hope into your circumstances?

Pray

God, when I feel at my wit's end, remind me that your presence and power change everything.

"God didn't promise to give you a painless way of life: He promised you a way of escape. He promised you help to bear your pain and to give you strength to put you back on your feet when weakness makes you stagger."

DAVID WILKERSON,
Have You Felt Like Giving Up Lately? Finding Hope and Healing When You Feel Discouraged

On Your Side

What shall we say about such wonderful things as these? If God is for us, who can ever be against us?

ROMANS 8:31 NLT

Pause

Anna lived with family while her house was being remodeled. One day she stopped by her house to talk with the contractors, and the police showed up. They told her that someone said she stole a package that had been delivered to that address.

Anna denied the accusation. She'd not received a package. Why would a stranger have used her address, anyway? The accuser pressed charges, and she had to go to court. If found guilty, she'd serve jail time. *Insanity.* Thankfully, Anna was vindicated, but the process was beyond stressful. Her only source of calm came in knowing that God was on her side.

God takes sides with all who place their faith in Jesus. In some cases, he proves their innocence. In other cases, evil seems to win. That doesn't mean he's taken sides with wrong. It means he's working behind the scenes, like he did in Joseph's life (Genesis 39). He's on our side to make us more Christlike and prepare us for purposes yet unseen.

Ponder

What evidence have you seen that God is on your side?

Pray

Father, I trust that you're on my side even when it doesn't appear so.

"The simple statement, 'God is for us,' is in truth one of the richest and weightiest utterances that the Bible contains."

J. I. PACKER,
Knowing God Devotional Journal:
A One-Year Guide

El Shaddai

In him our hearts rejoice, for we trust in his holy name.
May your unfailing love be with us, LORD,
even as we put our hope in you.

PSALM 33:21–22

Pause

Names are important. They're our identity. They're how others know us. The same is true about God's names—they're one way in which he reveals his identity to us. They're how we get to know him.

One of God's many names is El Shaddai. It means "God Almighty" and reminds us that he is all-powerful. The psalmist used it in Psalm 91:1—"Whoever dwells in the shelter of the Most High will rest in the shadow of the Almighty."

When life crumbles around us, we know we can find safety and solace in God Almighty's shadow. There's no better place to hide in times like this. He alone is our refuge. He alone provides the security for which we long when difficulties and disappointments come our way. He shields us from enemies such as fear and doubt and provides shade from the heat.

El Shaddai is there for us. He is our hope today and always.

Ponder

Psalm 91:1 reminds us of 911. We can call on El Shaddai for help. Bask in this truth.

Pray

Father, thank you for hiding me in your protective shadow. I will rest there.

"Faith is not believing in my own unshakable belief. Faith is believing an unshakable God when everything in me trembles and quakes."

BETH MOORE, *Praying God's Word: Breaking Free From Spiritual Strongholds*

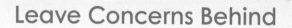

Leave Concerns Behind

Hannah was in deep anguish,
crying bitterly as she prayed to the LORD.

1 SAMUEL 1:10 NLT

Pause

Hannah lived in crisis for years before it finally reached a climax. While she'd been unable to conceive, her husband's other wife had borne several children and turned verbally and emotionally abusive toward her. It didn't help matters that her husband meant well but was clueless about why she felt so distraught.

In desperation, Hannah turned to God. She poured out her heart and held back nothing. "Then she went back and began to eat again, and she was no longer sad" (1 Samuel 1:18 NLT).

We might turn to God in our despair, too. We might give him our concerns like Hannah did. But sometimes we do something she didn't do. We say amen and then take our concerns back. For that reason, I don't welcome women to retreats with the words, "Leave your burdens at the door." The implication is that we'll pick them up and carry them with us when we head home. When we give God our problems, let's leave them with him.

Ponder

Cup your hands as if holding your difficult situation, and give it to the Lord.

Pray

Lord, please grant me the ability to leave my worries on your plate, not mine.

"May God remind us daily—no matter what obstacles we face—that we are loved and empowered by the One who brought the universe into existence with the mere sound of His voice. Nothing is impossible for Him."

BETH MOORE, *Praying God's Word: Breaking Free From Spiritual Strongholds*

Reflecting Jesus

"In the same way, let your light shine before others,
that they may see your good deeds
and glorify your Father in heaven."

MATTHEW 5:16

Pause

An elderly friend, Alf, fell on ice and broke his pelvis. Gene and I visited him in the hospital during his recovery. Kitchen staff brought lunch trays to him and his three roommates shortly after we arrived. Alf removed the cover from his plate to check out his meal: meatloaf a tad overcooked, mushy broccoli, and plain boiled potatoes. Canned fruit cocktail for dessert. Some folks might have grimaced, but not Alf. He smiled and said, "Thank you! I appreciate your kindness. This meal looks amazing." He spoke loud enough to ensure anyone within earshot could hear.

Alf sought to minister to others despite being in pain. When we arrived, he asked questions about our children and ministry. He looked out for his roommates' needs, and he thanked those who served him—doctors, nurses, kitchen staff, and janitors. He never uttered a complaint.

I don't know if Alf talked about Jesus in that place, but this I do know—he reflected Jesus to all who entered his room.

Ponder

How can you reflect Jesus in your current situation?

Pray

Lord, make me a channel of your blessing to others today. Let my attitudes and words show Jesus to others.

> "When trials expose our faith-life, will others see us embracing both the joy and the pain of our life? We do not need to live out one and deny the other. Those around us need to recognize that both of these elements are part of life, and both give us hope for heaven."
>
> KAY WARREN,
> *Choose Joy: Because Happiness Isn't Enough*

Give God the Controls

*Trust in the LORD forever, for the LORD,
the LORD himself, is the Rock eternal.*

ISAIAH 26:4

Pause

Gene and I flew to an indigenous community in northern Ontario to visit ministry coworkers. The copilot greeted us as we boarded the plane. In my humble opinion, he didn't look old enough to shave let alone fly a plane, but that didn't stop me from trusting him with my life. I knew nothing about this fellow or the pilot, but I didn't waste a second thought about letting them take the controls. They were, after all, running the show because they'd trained for the job.

If we trust strangers with our lives, how much more ought we to trust the Lord? Imagine—the God of everlasting strength holds us in his right hand. He carries us and comforts us and loves us so much that he sent his only son to pay our sin penalty with his life (John 3:16). Do you think we can trust him with our lives? I do. We ought to have no qualms about letting him take the controls.

Ponder

Are you okay with trusting God completely with your circumstances?

Pray

Lord of everlasting strength, help me yield all control into your capable hands.

"'You can have faith or you can have control, but you cannot have both.' If you want God to do something off the chart, you have to take your hands off the controls."

MARK BATTERSON,
*All In: You Are One Decision Away
From a Totally Different Life*

Overwhelming Victory

*No, despite all these things, overwhelming victory
is ours through Christ, who loved us.*

ROMANS 8:37 NLT

Pause

Olympic athletes wow us with their skills. I particularly enjoy watching downhill ski races. Tension runs high when four professional skiers compete for the gold, especially if it's a photo finish. Sometimes one one-hundredth of a second makes all the difference.

We're in a race, too. Our circumstances call us to run with perseverance and never give up. That sounds exhausting if not impossible, but here's the thing: God guarantees an overwhelming victory. We don't drag ourselves across the finish line. Neither do we end with a photo finish. We can finish strong because Christ says so: "I have told you all this so that you may have peace in me. Here on earth you will have many trials and sorrows. But take heart, because I have overcome the world" (John 16:33 NLT).

Isn't that a beautiful promise? Christ has overcome the world, and he lives in me and you. That means we're overcomers, too. No matter what we face, Christ in us leads us to an overwhelming victory!

Ponder

Bask in the joy of being invited to join Christ's winner's circle.

Pray

God, I trust you to accomplish the victory I desperately need today.

"I want to encourage you by letting you know that there's hope for you and your situation whatever you are dealing with. God is intimately involved with every detail of your future and His desire is for you to be an overcomer."

SUE AUGUSTINE,
When Your Past is Hurting Your Present:
Getting Beyond Fears That Hold You Back

Meet Grace

Grace is a devotional blogger, member of the First 5 writing team (Proverbs 31 Ministries), and popular speaker at women's retreats and conferences internationally.

Her passion is to connect the dots between faith and real life by helping her audiences learn to love, understand, and apply God's Word for life transformation. Besides writing and speaking, she's a career global worker and enjoys training others for short-term and career missions.

She and her husband, Gene, live on a sailboat near Vancouver, British Columbia.

www.gracefox.com
grace@gracefox.com
www.fb.com/gracefox.author